Spoiled

To Heather —
Be the rock!

Peggy Harper Lee

June 2012

Spoiled

Fresh Ideas for Parenting Your Entitled Child – at Any Age!

Peggy Harper Lee

ChickLit Media Group, Incorporated ● San Francisco

Published by ChickLit Media Group, Incorporated, San Francisco, California
Cover Design by Diedre Trudeau, ezeeye IMAGING Brand & Design Specialists
Author Photo by Gurpreet Kaur, Kaur Photography
Edited by Clare Price
Copy editing by Zoë Bird

Printed in the United States of America

ISBN 978-1-935598-83-1 paperback
ISBN 978-1-935598-07-7 Amazon ® Kindle ®
ISBN 978-1-935598-08-4 EPUB

First Paperback Edition

Dedication

To my children: Terryn, Alan, Timothy, and Owen.
You are enchanting and I love to see you soar.

Table of Contents

Foreword   1

Acknowledgements   5

Introduction   7

PART ONE: How Did I Get Here?   14

Chapter 1: Am I Spoiler Parent?   15

    Does This Sound Like You?   15

    Recognize and Acknowledge the Problem   18

    Roadblocks to Recognizing Spoiler Behavior   19

    What Are the Signs of a Spoiler Parent?   19

    Spoiling Can Happen at Any Age   20

    You Have to Fix Yourself, Not Fix Your Child   22

    Forgive Yourself   22

    OK, I Need to Change, but How?   23

    It Won't Be Easy, but It Will Be Worth It   24

Chapter 2: Is This Really My Child?   26

    Does This Sound Like Your Child?   26

    What Are the Signs of an Entitled Child?   29

The Entitled Child 0-10   30

Does Your Child Maintain Friendships Easily?   31

Do Relatives Comment on the Bad Behavior?   32

Are You Having the Same Conversation Again?   32

Does She Seem Unhappy?   33

Entitled Child 10-20   35

A Teen Can Control Her Demanding Behavior   37

Does She Seem Truly Grateful?   38

Is She Disrespectful?   39

Entitled Child 20+   39

Regardless of How Your Entitled Child Is...   42

Chapter 3: Dealing with the "Old Baggage"   44

Emotional Baggage from Childhood   47

What Does Baggage Do?   49

Freedom of Choice   51

Put the Baggage Down   52

Liz's Story   53

Chapter 4: How Did We Get Here?   56

Why Did I Not See This Coming?   59

Cloudy Vision   60

The Many Faces of Entitlement   61

Every Child Is Unique   62

What Do We Do When She's an Adult?   63

Chapter 5: My Circumstances Are Different   65

Common Challenges   65

No United Front   66

Divorce and the United Front   68

Grandparents Not in a Primary Parenting Role   72

Limited Resources   73

Lack of Confidence   75

Chapter 6: My Kid is Special   77

Each Child is Unique   78

Your Child is Defiant   82

Attention Seeking   84

Attempting to Gain Power and Control   85

Seeking Revenge   86

Acting Helpless   86

Your Child is Just Like You   87

Your Child is the Exact Opposite of You   88

She is Extremely Bright or Has Excessive Energy   89

The Risk of Unique Challenges   90

PART TWO: What Did I Do Wrong?   92

Chapter 7: Parent Power   93

How Do You Feel About Power?   93

How Did You Give Your Power Away?   96

A Child Doesn't Understand "Too Much of a Good
Thing"   97

Power Shift When Your Child Is an Adult   98

You Are in Charge Because You Are More Capable   100

Chapter 8: Think Before You Speak   101

Why Does This Happen?   102

Issues from Your Own Childhood Are Significant   103

You Are Currently Facing Significant Personal Issues   108

Your Child's Behavior Is Extreme   109

Pause - Pause Longer if You Are Upset   110

Chapter 9: Ignore It and It Will Go Away   111

I'm Doing the Best I Can   112

It's No Fun to Have to Say "No"   114

Chapter 10: I Want Her to Like Me   116

Strategies for When She Doesn't Agree   118

"You Don't Trust Me"   119

"You Don't Love Me"   121

She Questions Your Authority   122

Expect Her to Not Agree   123

Chapter 11: Really, It's Not That Bad   124

What Does Minimization Sound Like?   125

Minimization When Your Child Is 0-10   125

Minimization When Your Child Is 10-20   127

Minimization When Your Child Is 20+   128

How Do You Know if You Are Minimizing   129

Chapter 12: Her Happiness Is Everything to Me   133

Do You Love Her So Much You Are Hurting Her?   133

Are You Just Trying to Save Her from Herself?   136

PART THREE: What Do I Do Now?   140

Chapter 13: Kid Basics   141

Identify Family Values and Build Character 141

You Are a Powerful Teacher 143

Shower with Positive Attention to Reinforce Learning and Cooperation 144

How to Teach Without Being Preachy 145

Teach By Asking Questions Instead of Giving Answers 147

Use Humor Liberally 148

Have a Plan Before You Start 149

Chapter 14: Be the Rock 150

What Does It Look Like to "Be the Rock?" 151

Tools to Help you "Be the Rock" 152

The Power of "Oh" 152

Take a Deep Breath 153

Catch Her Being Wonderful 154

Show Her That You Are Calm and Reasonable 155

Chapter 15: Is This the Hill to Die On? 157

Consistency Is Not as Fun as Making Your Child Happy in the Moment 157

Just This Once 158

You Are Frustrated That Your Child Doesn't Listen and Comply 158

Your Lack of Consistency Has Led You to Conclude That Discipline Doesn't Work 159

Clear Expectations 160

Clear Consequences 164

Chapter 16: You Can't Have Your Cake and Wear Your Skinny Jeans Too 168

She Needs You to Set Boundaries 169

Cause and Effect 170

She May Not Always "Get It" at First 171

Cause and Effect When Your Child is 0-10 173

Cause and Effect When Your Child is 10-20 174

Cause and Effect When Your Child is 20+ 176

Chapter 17: Wait, Wait, It Will Be Great! 177

Why Help Him Tolerate Delayed Gratification 177

Curing the Gimmes 178

Instilling a Good Work Ethic 180

Learn to Tolerate Frustration 182

Take a Stand on Alcohol and Drugs 183

Teach Him to Wait 185

Chapter 18: Coping Skills That Make a Difference   187

Teach Her to Manage Frustration   188

Coping Skills   189

Avoid the Frustration   191

PART FOUR: A Word of Encouragement   194

Chapter 19: It's Worth it!   195

Important Reminders for Disciplined Parents   195

Your Child Needs You to Stop Spoiling Him   196

You Don't Need His Permission to Change from Spoiler to Disciplined Parent   198

Resources   200

About the Author   201

Connect with Me   202

Foreword

At just nine months old, my daughter was running my household. Here I had this beautiful baby, and all of a sudden she turned into a tyrant. At first I didn't even realize what had happened to our family. It was my dad who pointed out to my husband and me that we had a spoiled child. Once we realized that, we spent the next nine months undoing everything we had done before.

I was blessed with a thoughtful parent, my father, who had the courage to tell us that my daughter was running the household in time for us to fix it rather quickly. We did not stop cold turkey, but we did start to set some boundaries. We made minor shifts in how we did things. I learned that, sometimes, it's okay to let babies cry.

Peggy Harper Lee's book, *Spoiled*, is for parents like us; parents who may have unintentionally been on their way to creating an entitled child without realizing it, or have found themselves with an entitled child (at any age) and now know that they need to fix it. It's for moms who need to become empowered and dads who need to see that their children have their own, separate journeys. It's for all parents who need to learn how to respond instead of react when their kids challenge them.

The beauty of being human is that we do have the ability to change. We don't have to panic about it. We just have to set things up differently. Raising kids is a huge job. The only way you can write a book like *Spoiled* is while looking back; when you look back, you see your experience differently. Looking back over twenty-eight years of parenting, Peggy Harper Lee shares her no-nonsense approach and offers, finally, some relief for the parents of entitled children who feel they have tried everything else.

One thing I often see in us parents is the need to be liked by our kids. Most of our parents didn't care if we liked them. Today, we think our kids aren't going to like us but it's a myth and a lie. It keeps us from being effective parents. You cannot be your teenager's best friend. It is impossible. She needs her mom to step it up and be her mom. You will not have the authority or respect that you need to have when *she* needs it if you are her best friend. As Peggy says, "It's time to put on your big parent pants and take your power back; then you and your child will ultimately benefit."

All too often, an entitled child ends up in a therapist's office because he is completely confused about why the world isn't handing him everything on a silver platter. As the parent of an entitled child, you are probably inhibiting a lot of success in your child's life, because some of the things that shake our lives up are also the things that form us and give us our strengths. If the parent is writing the kid's essays and the kid is getting "A"s, how does that teach the kid to be a great student? It doesn't. You need to become empowered before you can empower your child.

An empowered mom really knows what her role is in her household. When a problem arises in the house, an empowered mom is very aware that no one else is going to take care of this problem. She's got to do it. An empowered mom listens to her own instincts.

An empowered mom knows how to handle her family in the way no one else does.

If you are not feeling empowered and you have an entitled child, the expectation level gets really high. The ante gets higher with pleaser parents who don't know how to lead. They overindulge to an excessive degree to make their kids' lives comfortable. In trying to make everybody happy, nobody is happy. And in reality, the people who are most content are the ones who don't expect to have everything. They don't expect a car on their sixteenth birthday. It doesn't mean that they are not highly exceptional people – it means that they are okay with things as they are.

As parents, we all want our children to be happy, to be grateful, and to find their own place in the world. An entitled child doesn't get that opportunity. No matter if your child is nine months old like my daughter was, or nine years old or even twenty-nine, there is still time to change your parenting skills – which will change your child's life for the better. The wisdom in *Spoiled* will help you get there.

Kristine Carlson is the author of three bestsellers:
Don't Sweat the Small Stuff in Love, Don't Sweat the Small Stuff for Women and *An Hour to Live, An Hour to Love: The True Story of the Best Gift Ever Given*. Her latest book, released April 2012 by Hyperion, is *Don't Sweat the Small Stuff for Moms*.

Acknowledgments

My deep gratitude goes to Adryenn Ashley, without whom this book would never have happened. Beyond being the flint to my steel, she kept the fire raging with her wit, insight and encouragement. Knowing her has greatly enriched my life.

Thank you also to Janice Niederhofer, who saw a spark, pointed me to Adryenn and cleared the background noise. Proceeding without chatter is a beautiful thing!

I am grateful beyond words to Clare Price, my editor, who could probably help me say it better than I just did. Clare, you are the perfect combination of insistent and encouraging, and through your thoughtful and intelligent input, this project is truly ready to meet the public.

I want to specifically thank my early readers and contributors for their feedback and spot-on observations. Your advice and support kept me going through the sometimes-painful editing process. You are a smart bunch, and you have all shared your time and resources with me so generously. I am blessed by the company I keep. Thank you to Stephanie Sherwood, Jen Riffe, Kari Hagensmith, Mary-Jo Meinhold, Phil Bodine, Tara McConnell, Janet Reiber, Janna

Woodroof, Julie Chafin, Cheryl Mullick, Kelly Peterson, Sandi Molash, Hollee Cummings, Michael Marsden, Kevin Hillburn and Danielle Graves.

So many others have been supportive, shared resources, and helped shove me when my momentum stalled. You know who you are, and I appreciate you.

Thank you to the professionals who helped with book mechanics: Stephanie Jensen, Gurpreet Kaur, Marie Hardy, Deidre Trudeau, Diane Perrine and A.J. Harper.

I have a very caring family, and I thank all of you for cheering me on.

Special thanks to my parents, Doyle and Rhonda Hanks, who are supportive of this book – even those parts that illuminate what would more comfortably be kept in the dark. They know the challenges of childrearing, and have enthusiastically embraced this project in the hopes that it will help other parents struggling with entitled children. I am proud to be your daughter and I know you are proud of me too.

Special love and gratitude goes to my four children, Terryn, Alan, Timmy, and Owen. Each of you fills a space in my heart that is dedicated solely to you. You remind me every day how lucky I am to be your mom.

And finally, to my husband Eeden – no woman could ever ask for a better partner. You have truly held down the fort, mended the breaks, fed the troops and kept the home-fires burning so that I could work on this project. This book is just as much your creation as it is mine. Thank you, my love.

Introduction

We live in the age of the Entitled Child. Many books have been written about entitlement and entitled children. This is not another one. This book, in contrast, is written for and about you: the parent of an entitled child.

You may know you have an entitled child and want to change your relationship with that child. You may be wondering if you have an entitled child and want to learn the signs of entitlement so you can be sure. You may have been warned that your child is in danger of becoming an entitled child. If so, this book is for you.

As we take this journey of the entitled child together, we'll examine what an entitled child looks, sounds and acts like at every stage from infancy to adulthood. We'll explore the strategies that you, as a parent, can use to effectively build a new relationship with your entitled child.

This book is designed to help parents struggling with entitled children in a generally healthy and loving home. There are issues that involve abuse, mental illness or other severe circumstances that should be addressed by medical, law enforcement or social services professionals and are outside the scope of this book.

So get ready to pull up your big parent pants and take back the power in your relationship and your home.

In our lifetime, the pendulum has swung from the extreme view that "children should be seen and not heard" to the opposite extreme, where many parents are almost literally placing the crown of entitlement on the baby's head at birth. We may, in our tenderhearted moments, think that the entitlement extreme is better than the "seen and not heard" extreme, but that's really not true.

Both have negative effects on our children, and both parenting styles can be devastating because both leave children feeling inadequate and confused.[1]

So what is the best approach? We need a new term; a new strategy; and a new tribe of parents looking to exercise appropriate power, be the everyday heroes and leaders that our children need us to be and refuse to make excuses for ourselves. We think of spoiled children as lacking discipline, and those from the "seen and not heard" era as being overly controlled. Perhaps being "disciplined," as applied to our parenting strategy, may bring us to the center – and together – in an effort to stem entitled and overindulged behavior. A disciplined parent will lead with purpose, vision, compassion, integrity, persistence and charisma. The power of our love for our children will likely take care of the desire and motivation to drive the change needed to curb the spoiling, provided that we as parents have the ability to recognize the problem as well as an idea of what to do about it.

This book is written to take you, the parent, on a journey. Don't worry: you don't have to be sure you are raising or have raised a

---

[1] Bredehoft, David J., Sheryll A. Mennicke, Alisa M Potter, Jean Illsley Clarke, "Perceptions Attributed By Adults To Parental Overindulgence During Childhood," *Journal of Family and Consumer Science Education*, vol. 16, no. 2 (Fall/Winter 1998): 12-14.

spoiled child, or be clear about whether your child is spoiled just a little or an awful lot before you start reading. The chapters in this book are organized to lead you in a progression that begins with awakening and realization. You need first to know where you are, to be clear about what has happened, and to understand that the pain you and your child are experiencing from spoiler parenting will likely get worse if you don't make some changes. Once you have that clarity, you will find guidance in starting to consider the solutions and tools needed to move to a disciplined parenting approach. This book offers help for special circumstances that might require more targeted strategies, as well as words of encouragement to help you stay dedicated to your new parenting approach.

First, know that you are not alone. Recent headlines confirm that the entitlement issue is huge and growing. As reported in the June 14, 2011 issue of SmartMoney magazine, a recent study by the National Endowment for Financial Education shows that 59% of parents support their adult children (ages eighteen to thirty-nine) who are not in college.[2] A 2008 article in WSJ.com, The Wall Street Journal's online magazine, titled "The 'Trophy Kids' Go To Work," looked at how the entitlement issue is impacting the workplace. In that piece, a survey by CareerBuilder.com was cited that showed 85% of hiring managers and human resource executives said they feel that the millennial generation (those born between 1980 and 2001) has a stronger sense of entitlement than older workers.[3] And the discussion around the U.S. Government's entitlement programs

---

[2] Anne Tergesen, "Are Your Kids Putting Your Retirement At Risk? Part II" *SmartMoney* Magazine (June 24, 2011), http://blogs.smartmoney.com/encore/2011/06/14/are-your-kids-puttingyour-retirement-at-risk-part-ii/ (accessed March 2, 2012).

[3] Adapted by The Wall Street Journal Online from a book from Ron Alsop, "The 'Trophy Kids' Go To Work," WSJ.com (October 21, 2008), http://www.wsj.com (accessed February 28, 2012).

have recently broken through some barriers that many long thought untouchable, as evidenced by the June 18, 2011 New York Times headline, "AARP says it's open to modest social security cuts."[4]

I am a financial advisor by profession, and I see the entitlement issue ruin financial security and strain marriages at an alarming rate. I work with individuals, families, and small businesses to help them identify, prioritize and achieve their financial goals and grow wealth. These plans are often derailed by ungrateful children – old enough to have children of their own – who are still draining their families' resources. I have had clients tell me that they can't possibly stop paying a cell phone bill or a car payment, or chipping in for rent for a grown child. The reasons vary, but they usually boil down to fear: fear that their child will be mad at them and withhold love, or fear that their child really can't succeed on his own and the related fear that this means they didn't do a good job as a parent.

Hearing my clients' stories, and seeing the devastation to family finances and relationships caused by entitled behavior, always broke my heart. And I often took off my financial advisor hat and became just a fellow parent, talking about strategies and solutions that clients could use to stop enabling their adult spoiled children. The tools and strategies I gave them worked, and they called me to report the positive progress. I began to see the patterns and notice that the mistakes my clients were making, the entitlement issues they were dealing with and the strategies to help them were all very consistent. And for most, it was not that difficult to make the changes needed to solve the problem. Knowing the pervasive nature of the entitlement issue, and that solutions could be made readily available and are relatively easy to implement, I became passionate about getting the

---

[4] Lichtblau, Eric, "AARP says it's open to modest social security cuts," New York Times, June 18, 2011: D-12.

help to more parents.

My clients are not the only ones with spoiled children. As a mom, I have volunteered for many parent and community organizations and have come face to face with entitled children and the parents who create them. One of my most memorable moments was while serving as the vice president of cheer for a community youth football league. One of my coaches was having difficulties with a nine year-old girl who consistently ignored directions, refused to participate in exercises and missed several practices. I spoke to her mother and explained the situation, the negative effect it was having on morale and how it was hurting the team's ability to perform routines. I was hoping for her help and was very shocked by her response. She said, "I can't believe you people. You expect too much. If my daughter doesn't want to do something, then she doesn't have to do it." I later learned that this same mother had refused to meet with her older son's history teacher because it conflicted with her manicure appointment.

We see these children everywhere, screaming through restaurants, playing with cell phones in the movie theater and ignoring authority figures. Then they grow up and enter the workplace, get into romantic relationships and spend money. If they are entitled, they are not equipped to do any of those things well; and the damage to others and society in general is tremendous. I am not the first to notice the entitlement issue, nor the first to start a conversation on how to solve it. However, I know that to have any chance at change we have to start at the beginning – which means that, as parents, we have to stand up and say no.

I am writing this book as a mom with real-world experiences. I have four children of my own, ranging in age from three to twenty-eight. I can relate to the highs and lows of parenting. I know that those of us in the trenches can sometimes feel like trying our best isn't enough. I've been there; and through this book, I hope to connect with other parents as passionate about the entitlement issue as I am, to help people learn from the mistakes of others and to help parents find solutions.

How am I different from other parents, particularly the ones struggling with entitled children? The reality is, I am not all that different. Like any mom, I would throw myself in front of a bus to save my child. I get frustrated with obnoxious behavior, and I am sometimes weary and overwhelmed with the demands of rearing my children.

However, I am also a trailblazer. When something is not working, I search for answers and try new approaches until I find one that does work. I am not afraid to try something that seems counterintuitive, or to reach out for help. I also realize that I have choices. I can choose to model the methods my parents used, do the exact opposite, or find another path. Somehow, I intuitively know that I have to keep my baggage away from my children or risk damaging them with it.

If you know or suspect you are dealing with entitled children, the good news is that you created it, so you can fix it. There are different strategies that you will need to use, depending on the age of your child, but it's never too early or too late to cure the entitlement monster. Here's the catch. You knew there was going to be one! You have to fix you, not your child. Your child, whether over or under the age of eighteen, will learn what you have to teach so long as you have a serviceable parent-child relationship. You need to teach differently. To be able to do that, you need to change your way of thinking. You provide the will and I'll help with the way.

To talk about children, I have used the pronouns he and she, alternating by chapter. I know that really cute and equally monstrous behavior is not limited to one gender and have used this alternating approach both to be fair and to facilitate the writing. If you like, feel free to substitute the gender of the child in your life.

Part One

How Did I get Here?

1

Am I a Spoiler Parent?

Does This Sound Like You?

My client, Jack, is very upset. He is sitting in my office telling me his story, and it's one that I hear over and over.

My married daughter calls. It's an emergency. "Could you and Mom please come for dinner tonight?" She will cook. I just need to drive the 120 miles in rush hour traffic. I rearrange my plans for the evening, run the dizzying list of possible horrors that could have happened through my mind, and make a mental note to stop for gas on the way. My daughter is twenty-eight, been married for three years, her family's income is north of $200,000, she just had my first grandchild six months ago and as far as I know the marriage is good. The waiting is agony, but she would not discuss the emergency on the phone except to say that nobody's sick.

Pleasantries have barely been exchanged before my daughter can stand it no longer. She is in obvious distress and decides to just come straight to the point. "Daddy," she wails, "Aidan's preschool is *going to cost $25,000, and we don't have the money to pay for it."*

I sit quietly, thinking that the bad news is still coming. I feel empathy because my daughter is in pain, but I'm still trying to connect that level of distress with the news she just delivered. Tragedy is in the eye of the beholder, but Aidan hasn't even started to crawl or cut a tooth and the last I checked, annual tuition at a decent university is less than $25,000. While trying to clear the confusion in my head, I notice that my daughter, son-in-law and wife are all looking at me expectantly. I wonder, do they actually think that this is where I pull out my checkbook and console my daughter for this injustice with cash?

As I listen to Jack's story, I struggle with my own mixed emotions. First, because it didn't happen to me, it is almost funny. Here we have a married woman and mother who is apparently incapable of distinguishing between a want and a need. Her sense of entitlement is so enormous that she doesn't hesitate to ask Daddy and Mommy to pay the preschool tuition bill. And what kind of man did she marry who would just sit there silently while his wife pleads financial hardship to her parents to solve this kind of a problem?

Second, the story is incredibly sad. Here's Jack, whose household income is about half of his daughter's; he is having his own debt issues, is less than ten years from retirement, and will probably be working long past the time when he should have been able to step away from the daily grind. He is still giving money to his adult children just because they ask. In trying to give them everything they want and make them happy, he has crippled them. With the best of intentions, he has taught them that they are entitled to instant gratification and that they don't have to solve their own problems.

My job here is to help my client. I have been working with Jack for over a year, trying to help him understand that he shouldn't still be financially supporting his three children – who are all college graduates – both for his sake and for theirs. I would like to take all the credit for making progress with him by helping him to understand how important it was that he refused to write a check for the tuition on the spot; but his daughter helped me out by making a request so outrageous that, for the first time, Jack didn't immediately comply. Now he's starting to get angry. The smaller amounts didn't seem like such a big deal, but this latest request has him feeling taken for granted. I spend the next half hour helping him understand that it's all connected. How could he think that he could constantly give in to her demands for the smaller stuff, and that she would be mature enough not to ask for the bigger stuff?

I ask Jack some key questions: What would it have meant to his family if he had recognized the entitlement monster when his girl was very young? Would she now be more independent and resourceful? Is this affecting her happiness, because she always wants more than she can provide for herself? And how is this going to affect Aidan, his granddaughter?

The role-modeling Jack provided is not the kind he wants to see repeated with another generation. Jack is starting to realize that he is now facing the crux of the entitlement issue. We all would love to have our cake and eat it too. However, for every entitled person taking a short cut, someone else has to pay the bill, carry the weight, or take up the slack. He now recognizes the entitlement issue is the problem and is ready to tackle it head-on.

Recognize and Acknowledge the Problem

Jack was very resistant to the idea that his children were entitled, and until his daughter asked for the $25,000, he was still not facing the truth. He tended to minimize the degree of his daughter's entitlement, rationalizing that only the children who threw screaming fits, acted disrespectfully to their parents and had trouble in school were the ones who really had the problem.

The reality is, Jack is what I like to call a "spoiler parent." Although intensity and specifics vary greatly, all spoiler parents have three characteristics in common. These parents partially or completely relinquish their power to the child, expect too little from the child, and allow personal issues to interfere with effective parenting.

Jack's own childhood was harsh and without luxury. When his daughter was born, his goal was to make life easier for her than what he had experienced. To protect himself from his own discomfort, he shielded her from frustration and gave her privileges she did not earn.

Like Jack, every parent who is dealing with an entitled child has to go through an awakening process before the problem can be addressed. However, no parent wants to admit that their child behaves in an entitled manner or that their own mistakes created the problem.

Until you are clear what the issue is and are willing to acknowledge it, you cannot correct it. If you are reading this book, you may have the sense that something is wrong and you need to do something about it. If you are still having difficulty acknowledging that your child has an entitlement issue, see if you can identify with one of the common reasons other parents have also struggled.

Roadblocks to Recognizing Spoiler Behavior

1) Lack of knowledge or clarity about what entitled behavior looks like

2) Reluctance to acknowledge or even consider the problem due to personal issues or baggage, including fear and guilt

3) Minimizing the degree of the behaviors and therefore rationalizing that they don't need to be addressed

4) Reluctance to acknowledge the problem because admitting it means that something needs to be done that the parent is not willing or equipped to handle

5) Reluctance to acknowledge the problem in an effort to avoid admitting that the parent has made mistakes and caused the child pain as a result

If you identify with one of these roadblocks, I'm glad you are here. We will address each of these in detail as we go through the journey from spoiler to disciplined parent. At this point, just acknowledging the problem and making the commitment to move forward is all you need to do.

What Are the Signs of a Spoiler Parent?

You may be asking, "What does a spoiler parent look like, and how will I know if that's me?" No one has an exhaustive list, and there are qualities that would seem opposite that actually have the same effect. For example, an overprotective parent who never lets a child experience disappointment or frustration can create an entitled child, just as an over-permissive parent can. If you are struggling with the entitlement monster, you will most likely identify with at least one of the traits below:

1) Your discipline is inconsistent

2) You crave your child's approval

3) You are overprotective

4) You get frustrated often and respond to your child in a reactive manner

5) You are overindulgent

6) You are weak

7) You are afraid to let your child make mistakes or experience consequences of his actions

8) You make decisions based on personal fear or guilt versus what is best for your child

9) You rescue your child from his own mistakes

10) You expect too little from your child

11) You are over-permissive

Spoiling Can Happen At Any Age

It doesn't matter how old your child is. Spoiler parenting behavior can begin at any stage. Even if you have successfully negotiated the terrible twos, you still have the potential to spoil your child. Some parents are rock solid on setting limits and being consistent with their toddlers, and then start to falter once their child builds vocabulary and learns to charm and cast spells. This is not evil or deliberately manipulative behavior; it's how your child tests boundaries, and your response teaches him how to behave. Being blinded by the cuteness haze is understandable, but not in the best interest of your child; and if you don't catch it in the early stages, you will spoil him.

Other parents lose it at the teenage phase. Let's face it, we all lose it at some point when dealing with teenagers. But consistently losing it and giving in to your teenager will not prepare him for a world that doesn't really care how bright and funny and handsome he is if he's behaving in a self-centered, lazy or disrespectful way.

Whatever stage of the game, the problem doesn't really seem to be a problem at first glance. You want your child to be happy and protected from danger, pain and disappointment. Nothing wrong with that. Period. What's the difficulty, then? Just make sure he has everything he wants, when he wants it, in the amount he wants, whether it's good for him or not – oh, wait, this isn't sounding so good anymore. And, how do you feel when he is metaphorically opening his beak and waiting to be fed pre-digested worms in your nest at the age of thirty-two, with a child of his own that also wants to be fed?

That's why you can't just protect your child and make sure he doesn't experience frustration and pain. If you do, he will learn to expect handouts that the world isn't going to give him. Not that pain or frustration are good, but he needs to experience them to learn how to deal with them and make good choices for himself. You can't be there to save him all the time when he's a child, and your ability to always be there declines as he grows. Once he's an adult, you won't want to be there constantly to save him – trust me on this, even if it seems like a good idea while you're still dazed with cuteness.

It helps to understand that you can't possibly be an umbrella over him for his entire life, and that the best way to protect him as much as you can is to prepare him to protect himself. If you have raised or are raising an entitled child, you are loving him so much that you are hurting him.

You Have to Fix Yourself, Not Your Child

If you find yourself asking, "Why does my child make outrageous demands, create havoc, act disrespectful, get easily frustrated and seem always to be taking the easy way out?" here's the answer: you taught him.

You taught him to expect you to bail him out and make his life easy. Now you're not happy with the results of that strategy. He has missed out on developing some important life skills, and the sad truth is that he is not really happy, either. Nothing is going to change if you simply tell him to behave differently, because your child doesn't believe you. Nothing terrible is going to happen if he doesn't get a job and take responsibility for himself, because you have always taken care of him – and, in his mind, you always will.

The good news is that you created it; you can fix it. Here's the catch – and you knew there was going to be one – you have to fix you, not your child. There are different strategies that you will need to use depending on the age of your child, but it's never too early and never too late to cure the entitlement monster. Your child, no matter his age, will learn what you have to teach as long as you have a serviceable parent-child relationship. You need to teach differently. To be able to do that, you need to change your way of thinking. You provide the will, and this book will help with the way.

Forgive Yourself

The path begins with you. The most important step is to forgive yourself. You did not intend to create an entitled child. Instead, your motivation has been to make sure your child is loved and cared for.

No excuses are necessary. The sooner you can forgive yourself, the sooner you can move forward and change. If you were raised as an entitled child, you may need to forgive your parents. They are not responsible for what has happened in your home, but not having a good role model certainly made your path more difficult.

You have the power to un-spoil. Frustrated parents often underestimate their power. Your efforts at curbing entitled behavior may not be working, but that only means that the methods are not working, not that you don't have tremendous ability to influence your child. You'll need to be free from guilt and fear to do so. We're all responsible for what we've done to our children, even the fantastic things. This is not the time to feel guilty about everything, but rather the time to focus on what you can change and make better.

Okay, I Need to Change, but How?

Your child was not born spoiled. Most parents struggling with entitled children know this on some level, but it's still hard to hear and even harder to accept. It's difficult to acknowledge that you started with a baby so full of promise and, often with the best of intentions, have ended up with a demanding, ungrateful, needy person.

But this not about your child. This is all about you. You need to spend some time, get very honest with yourself and figure out what it is about you that needs to change. Is it feeling guilt or fear, being overwhelmed, not having the correct tools or a combination of all those things that has contributed to your parenting in a way that has created an entitled child?

The truth is that your decisions and parenting have provided fertile ground for the entitlement monster to grow and flourish. You have created something that is the exact opposite of what you intended. Your decisions have hurt your child, but you can make new decisions that will help him now. You need to be his parent, not his friend. Parents love unconditionally, are willing to make great sacrifices and unselfishly use their time and talents to provide for their children. Why would you want to just be your child's friend when you could be so much more – his parent?

You can make new decisions. You can change yourself. You have the power to be a different kind of parent to your child. This is about you, because the only person you can change is yourself. You can't change your child. He's going to be influenced by the changes you make. Depending on how old he is now, he will be able to develop the skills he needs to be more grateful and self-reliant quickly or more slowly; but he's in charge of himself, just as you're in charge of you. This is about you, and you will need to remember that because there will be plenty of frustrating moments. You have to change what you can control and trust that the decisions you are making will be of ultimate benefit to your child. If you "fixed" your child and didn't change your parenting, you would just re-spoil him. If you fix yourself and he's still a minor, he has a chance to learn what he needs to be enchanting. If he's an adult, he'll learn that you still love him but aren't going to enable his entitled behavior anymore, which will hopefully give him the spark he needs to begin making some positive changes of his own.

It Won't Be Easy, but It Will Be Worth It

Now that you have recognized that you are a spoiler parent, you may be experiencing some painful and overwhelming emotions because you are admitting that you may have made some mistakes in parenting. Here is where many parents stay in the comfort of the known instead of being willing to risk the unknown.

Often in life, we wait to take action until the pain we are experiencing exceeds a threshold we are willing to bear. Your entitled child is already in a lot of pain, but that's not something you can accurately recognize or fully appreciate. I'm talking about your pain. You may be feeling sad, angry or frustrated because your child is coming to you to be rescued. However, your sense of guilt or your love for your child may still be keeping you stuck. The realization that your child is pampered and ill-equipped to take care of himself now or later in the adult world is frightening, and can provide the inspiration to overcome whatever is keeping you stuck.

2

Is This Really My Child?

Does This Sound Like Your Child?

We were never going to be "that mother" or "that father." If we thought we were going to fail as parents, we may never have willingly conceived. We have a natural tendency to minimize our own child's bad behavior, or rationalize it away as being normal or average, to avoid having to face our own shortcomings. It's natural to protect ourselves emotionally from the possibilities that we are a "bad parent" or have a "bad child."

One of the most outrageous examples I've seen of a child behaving badly happened when my oldest son was ten years old, and I was attending his baseball game. I was sitting on the bench with the other moms, chatting away as the team warmed up, when one of the other players walked over to his mom to find some Gatorade. After searching the bag that was near her and not finding any, he looked at her and demanded, "Mom, where is my Gatorade?" She quickly explained that she had forgotten to put it in the bag, and that she was sorry. He looked her straight in the eye and said, "You're so stupid, Mom. How could you forget it again? You need to go get some right now." It was no surprise, given that this child felt so comfortable berating his mother in a public setting, that she grabbed her purse and ran to the store after asking him what flavor he preferred.

This child's behavior was mortifying; and his mother's reaction was so unusual that it seemed inconceivable she had witnessed the same behavior the rest of us had. I remember the uncomfortable-to-angry looks the other mothers and I exchanged. We all instinctively knew not to comment. As bad as this child's behavior was, it was clear that his mother was either oblivious or in complete denial and making a comment would only serve to inflame the situation.

But what about a less extreme example? I was on a three-hour flight returning to the West Coast while in the seat behind me, a four year-old child kicked my seat constantly. After an hour that seemed more like ten, I politely asked the mother and father flanking the squirmy guy for assistance. His dad was uncomfortable, and looked to the child's mom to handle the situation. She told me, in a very weak voice, that he was only four and it couldn't be helped. In her world, four year-olds kick and she was helpless to do anything about it. Based on her response, I knew that there was little I could say to help her recognize that her child was misbehaving and could reasonably be expected to stop kicking. Her response would likely have been to defend her child, or to take it one step further and attack me. Not wanting an ugly or pointless confrontation, I asked to be reseated. His parents and I all catered to his behavior, and his parents failed to teach him about etiquette or to set clear and reasonable expectations for him. What's worse is that they didn't even try.

In not teaching kids, we are actually teaching them volumes. The boy on the plane learned that his behavior would be tolerated, even if objectionable to other adults. That's a lot of power – and he was already learning how to use it to manipulate others.

Whether her behavior is that extreme or subtler, your child is brilliant and crafty and doing exactly what she learned to do. You taught her. It doesn't matter whether your lessons were intentional or acts of omission. Both are powerful, and it's often what you don't say that speaks the loudest to your child.

It's easier to recognize the entitled child when you see one in another home, or out in public. Your friend has a four year-old who cries non-stop throughout the day. You can't even have a pleasant conversation with her without multiple interruptions and negotiations with this child who just can't be placated. You have another friend who bought a new car for the second time in three weeks, for her teenage son who drives like a maniac and totaled the first car. You know someone with a twenty-five year-old son living at home who is not working and doesn't pay any of his own bills. Each day he rises around noon, eats, plays video games, goes out with friends and stays out late.

You knew you had some issues, but just weren't willing to accept that your child had become an entitled monster because she never seemed as bad as the really spoiled kids. Now that you are ready to recognize it in your own child – as painful as that may be – this can at least give you some hope that things can be different.

Recognizing the bad behavior in your own child is not pleasant. It's always easier to see it in some else's child. You don't love their child to pieces, so you can view selfish behavior and label it for what it is without the rationalization. You may choose to end a play date early when your friend's child is cranky and hitting other children. On the ride home, you may be thinking about cutting back on play dates with that child because he often seems to be out of control and aggressive with the other kids. Your thought process may be very different if it is your own daughter creating the chaos. You might be thinking that you need to adjust her nap-time on play date Thursdays, or that maybe this group of kids isn't the best mix for her.

What Are the Signs of an Entitled Child?

While you may have the sense that your child is entitled, you may also be wondering, "What does an entitled child look like, and how will I know if my child is one?" Just as with the characteristics of the spoiler parent, there is no exhaustive list, and there are qualities that would seem counterintuitive. For example, an overindulged child who seemingly wants for nothing will typically be unhappy. The list below includes traits that are common to entitled kids of all ages, as well as some that are more age-specific.

1) Your child's behavior in public is embarrassing
2) She is relentless, repeating bad behavior until she gets her way
3) You have the same argument over and over again
4) Your child is often unhappy
5) You get comments from friends and family about how they would not have been allowed to behave that way
6) You often say "just this once"
7) Your child lacks gratitude and is hard to please
8) She plays one parent against the other
9) She lacks the ability to delay gratification

10) She expects privileges without responsibilities

11) She is self-medicating to control her frustration, anger or anxiety

12) She is unmotivated and performing below her capabilities

13) She asks to or expects to be rescued

14) She lacks sustained effort

15) She complains that you don't trust her

The Entitled Child 0-10

A list is helpful in identifying an entitled child, but there are some variations by age group that can throw parents off. Getting clear on some of the nuances is helpful.

It's probably most difficult to recognize the behavior of an entitled child when she is very young. You are still figuring out your child's temperament, how she relates to the world, what her strengths and weaknesses are and how you can best guide her. You may likely be able to overlook her entitled behavior, and make excuses for her public bad behavior by pointing out that she's just precocious. At some point, you may be increasingly embarrassed by her antics or even begin to avoid public or group activities.

How do you recognize an entitlement problem in a child under ten? Here are four critical questions that will help you recognize whether or not you are raising an entitled child:

1) Does your child maintain friendships easily?

2) Do relatives comment on her bad behavior?

3) Are you having the same conversation again and again?

4) Does she seem unhappy?

Does Your Child Maintain Friendships Easily?

Does she have friends who want to play with her? Do her friends' parents love to have your child over? Is she polite, courteous, and a joy to be with? If not, you're not likely to hear about it. Your child just won't get many play date invitations. If your child is not getting invited over to play with her friends, have you wondered why not? What if your child refuses to share, and is demanding and disrespectful in other people's homes? Have you asked? Of course, there may be other reasons you have to make the all the play dates. It may be that you are more organized, the other children's parents work and are busy, or you have the best playroom on the block. But you need to ask the other parents why and seek honest answers.

Your child may play well with others in your home, and even have successful play dates, but struggle with maintaining friendships at school where there is less direct supervision. Does she complain that she feels left out or that no one is nice to her? Her teacher can be a good source of information. She will be able to tell you if your child seems to be having fun and is able to join in with different groups of kids, or if she is hanging back and finding solitary activities to occupy her time. If she's on her own, it may be because other kids know how to spot an entitled child and won't be friends with one. An eight year-old child has no incentive or interest in making sure the demands of another child are met. A one-way street is no fun, and other kids won't put up with it. There's no peer cuteness haze. If you hear about problems and have ruled out other developmental, medical, or social issues and your child complains that no one wants to play with her or be her friend, you likely have an entitled child.

Do Relatives Comment on Her Bad Behavior?

Relatives, especially grandparents, may be very direct and criticize you for spoiling your child. Others will make comments like, "My mom would have killed me if I acted like that," or "That wasn't allowed in our house when I was growing up." If you are hearing comments like these from relatives, they may be seeing something that you are not. Although the comments may hurt and could be delivered more appropriately, find the truth in what they are trying to communicate. You may be too close to the situation and could benefit from an outsider's point of view.

Are You Having the Same Conversation Again?

If you are having the same conversations with your child over and over and nothing is changing, you may be dealing with and reinforcing the behavior of an entitled child. This pattern of continued confrontation indicates that your child has learned she will eventually get what she wants – either because you give in or because you stop paying attention.

For example, your child wants to wear the same shirt to school every day because it's the only one she owns that's cool and doesn't have a scratchy tag on it. You have purchased more shirts (some of them are tag-less), cut tags out and taped over seams, tried to reason with your child to expand her definition of cool, all to no avail.

Occasionally you see her with a random shirt on, but for the most part she goes to school every day in that Oregon Ducks t-shirt that her grandfather gave her for Christmas. You rationalize that at least it's dark green and doesn't show the dirt like her lighter shirts. And it is special to her because it's from her grandfather. Is it really so bad that she wears one shirt every day of her life? She doesn't sweat yet, so it doesn't smell too bad. You let her do it several days in a row and then ask her to change on the fourth day. She cries, says she can't go to school now, and with five seconds to spare, you run out the door to get her to school on time and... she's still an Oregon Duck. On the fifth day, as you are busy with breakfast and the other kids, the Duck goes out the door on the way to school unnoticed. Pretty soon the Duck shirt hasn't made it to the laundry pile in a few weeks. Finally, you start up the conversation again – with the same result, because your child is going to argue until you give in. You are reinforcing her entitled behavior.

It's not about the shirt, or whatever the conversation seems to be about. You may not have a problem with a mono-shirt child, so you decide to wash the shirt every other day and choose other battles. However, if you have decided that your child cannot wear the same shirt to school every day, then it is up to you to make sure that your wishes are followed. If you choose the battle, you have to follow through or you teach her that she can ignore you and do whatever she pleases.

Does She Seem Unhappy?

An unhappy child is often an entitled child. This sounds counterintuitive, but it's true. A child who expects every want to be fulfilled is going to be frustrated a lot more than a child who understands that she is loved and well-cared for but will not get everything she wants. Some entitled children are whiny and demanding only with their parents, some only with peers and friends, and some with everyone. Giving in to a child's demands in an effort to make her happy reinforces the behavior and provides only a brief period of relief.

I have a friend whose son, Josh, is easily frustrated and whines and cries often. She had a project to accomplish that required a great deal of concentration, and couldn't get it done with Josh's constant interruptions. She asked me to help her, and bring my son over with me so he could hopefully provide enough distraction for Josh that we could get the job done.

It didn't even take five minutes for Josh to start acting up. He was in and out of the room for over thirty minutes, carrying on about not being able to find a balloon launcher that he wanted to play with. My son tired of Josh's antics quickly and went outside to play in the pool by himself.

Having had countless conversations with my friend about her son's behavior, I decided not to say anything and just observe how she handled the situation. She did nothing for a very long time. Josh whined, tugged on his mother's arm and threw a tantrum, all while she ignored him and kept working. After about thirty minutes she looked up as if hearing him for the first time, asked him what was wrong, then went with him and found the balloon launcher where he had left it in the garage. He was happy for about twenty minutes – until he got frustrated that my son was playing with his football and started whining for his mother to get it back for him. Eventually, she tired of his whining again, found another ball and traded it with my son so that Josh could have the ball he wanted.

Because Josh has been overindulged, he is easily frustrated. He's not happy, and no one around him is happy either.

The Entitled Child 10-20

There's nothing like the magic of a special event to bring out the worst in an entitled teenager. My friend's daughter, Samantha, was going to prom with her boyfriend of three months. Deeply in love, Samantha was determined to create the perfect prom experience. Her bank account was tiny, but her dreams were immense. She wanted a limousine, an expensive dress, an after-party at the beach with her friends and a photographer to record the event. The price tag for her dreams grew to over $10,000. Of course, she wasn't going to pay the tab.

Sara and Jim, Samantha's parents, were financially comfortable and could easily afford $10,000. They were somewhat concerned about spoiling her, but also worried about disappointing her and crushing her dreams. During the decision-making process, Samantha pulled out all the stops. She alternated between extremely charming and cooperative behavior and manipulative tantrums. She was determined and relentless, and eventually wore down her parents. Sara and Jim agreed to pay for the dress, limousine, beach party and professional photographer. Samantha had a wonderful time, broke up with her boyfriend that same weekend, and resented her parents for insisting that they supervise the beach party. After spending over $10,000, they were hoping for a better outcome.

The teenage years are difficult for every parent-child relationship, but these issues are magnified when dealing with an entitled child. At this age, your child is now as big as or bigger than you are. You may also feel like it's been a long battle and that you may lose simply from exhaustion. An entitled teenager is not as subtle as his twenty-something counterparts or as cute as the under-ten crowd. This is when you are likely to confirm your growing suspicions that you have created a monster that you don't really like.

Like many parents of entitled teens, you may have adopted a survival mindset that you think will help you endure the teenage years. You may think that maturity and reasonable behavior will kick in once your child becomes an adult. This is not true, but it may be the only thought keeping you sane.

Now the demanding and ungrateful behavior is in high gear, and you are unaffected by the cuteness haze. Your child doesn't bother to throw in that you are the best mom ever, and crawling up into your lap to give you a hug is now difficult due to her size. The looks you get now involve eye-rolling. At this stage the battles really begin, especially if you have recognized the entitlement monster and have started trying to make some changes to curb the behavior. And battles at this stage are fierce, since your child will do whatever she can to make sure you don't stop the gravy train.

Your child's survival strategy is really all about preserving the status quo. She likes getting her way and doesn't want you to change a thing. This means she really has to work you over if you are trying to deny her what she wants. For example, she may change things up by creating a drama over something she really doesn't care about so she can give in this time – and then use that as justification for the next twenty times that she doesn't want to give in. It will go something like, "See Mom, I never get to do what I want. You made me go to the family reunion, which was so boring, but I went anyway and now you won't let me hang out at the mall with my friends on Saturday. It's not fair!" This back and forth exchange is exhausting, and the entitled teen has the skills, energy and determination at this stage of the game to win.

A Teen Can Control Her Demanding Behavior

An entitled teenager will not have the same problems keeping friends or being included that she did as a younger child. She has learned that getting what she wants requires different strategies depending on the audience. Teachers are generally to be ignored and avoided. Sadly, children today understand that teachers have little power, so avoiding consequences from a teacher is simple for the junior and senior high school crowd.

Friends and peers require more work and strategy. Your daughter knows she cannot demand $20 from a friend, pitch a fit if she doesn't get it, and expect that friend to even talk to her the next day. However, she can make the same demand for $20 from you, and regardless of whether you give in to her that day or not, she knows you will still continue to love her, feed her and provide for her needs. As a teen, your child has learned how to get what she wants by using techniques tailored to whomever has what she wants.

The other two major entitlement issues haven't changed much. You are still having the same conversations over and over again with her. It's just that the subjects of the conversations are different. Now you're not in conflict over candy and shorts in cold weather, it's about money and curfew. Your relatives, if they are really brave, are still telling you that they would have been killed if they behaved the way your daughter does. Your child is still very unhappy, although the ultra-spoiled child could appear happy since she doesn't have to engage in much conflict to get everything she wants.

All children will say, "But everyone else gets to do it" and "I'm the only one who doesn't have one." So how do you determine whether it's the entitlement monster or normal teen behavior? You will know because an entitled teen will have developed some beliefs and values that support her way of interacting with the world.

Does She Seem Truly Grateful?

One of the biggest clues is that the entitled child will lack gratitude. She will say thank you, particularly to people other than her parents, but with a lack of emotion or sincere gratitude. Why should she appreciate something that she deserves, needs and is entitled to? If it's expected, then it's harder to be thankful for.

How will you know that she's not truly grateful? If she's gotten exactly what she wants, she will be happy, but that's not the same as grateful. It's an important distinction. Gratitude is an emotion that comes from a humble place, and is an expression of appreciation for another's effort or sacrifice. One can be grateful even if the situation or outcome is not ideal.

An entitled child will have an expectation set in advance. The outcome will be judged against the expectation, leaving her frustrated if it is less than what she wanted and merely satisfied if the expectation is met.

And what if you have made a compromise? For example, you go to the mall with a $50 budget for jeans, but the pair she falls in love with are $150. You decide that you will stretch your budget to $80 and buy her the jeans that are her second choice. Is she happy to have a nice pair of jeans, or is she still fuming that she didn't get the more expensive ones? Body language and tone of voice will tell the real story.

Is She Disrespectful?

This feeds into the next – and maybe biggest – issue parents of an entitled teen struggle with: disrespectful behavior. Again, all teens will be ill-mannered on their journey from young childhood to adulthood; what is different in the entitled child is the degree and frequency of bad behavior. This comes from the beliefs and values of your child. If she is entitled, she will feel wronged and disrespected when she is denied a want or is disciplined for an inappropriate behavior. She doesn't yet have the skills to handle herself responsibly, so she retaliates with even more disrespect. She may know that two wrongs don't make a right, but lacks the maturity to control her actions. This is often an eye-opener for parents. Appropriately disciplining your child is not disrespectful, but if your daughter views it that way she will respond accordingly. Disrespect is her reality, and she will dish it back because she feels justified.

The Entitled Child 20+

You have finally made it to high school graduation and one last summer of playing and fun. Your entitled child may be a little easier to separate from when she goes off to college, because you will gladly take some moments of peace and quiet. However, you may also understand that she lacks the skills to succeed outside of your home, so the worry factor will now kick in to overdrive and ultimately rob you of your peace. Many entitled children won't leave for college, so you'll now have the worry and the surly attitude to deal with on a daily basis. What happened? Wasn't this the day you waited for? Wasn't this when you thought you could relax a little, knowing that your day-to-day parenting duties were over and that your child could now function independently and responsibly? Herein lies the problem. She doesn't have all the skills she needs to succeed as an adult; and, even worse, she doesn't have any desire to develop them or be responsible for herself. You have made it too easy to be greedy and dependent.

As mentioned before, the adult entitled child has the advantage of subtlety. She is also usually very skilled at playing to your weakness. If guilt is your weakness, be prepared for a nuclear war once you decide to cut off the gravy train.

Once your child was "on her own," you thought she would take care of herself. Now it is clear that she is still relying on you to take care of some of her basic needs, you can no longer deny that she is spoiled and perfectly comfortable with letting you provide for her.

The entitled child in her twenties always needs something from you. For almost every entitled child, it's some form of financial assistance, even if she is college-educated and has a well paying job. This goes for the child in her thirties, forties, fifties and beyond if you are still enabling the behavior.

The adult entitled child also tends to be lazy or unmotivated. She wants the college education, a great career and a family of her own, but is unwilling to put forth the effort it takes to achieve these things. You are no longer able to give her everything. You can't run your own adult life and hers too. When she was still a minor, this strategy worked, but you can't possibly hand her a great job, a degree and a stable relationship.

Sadly, because she is unable to cope with the ups and downs of normal adult life, the entitled adult child may self-medicate. Whether it's disengaging through video games or checking out with the help of alcohol or drugs, the entitled adult child often compounds the problems of underachievement by burdening herself with problems that will greatly impact her ability to contribute to society as a responsible adult. If this happens, it will put further strain on your relationship as you struggle to help her find success and make good choices while she becomes less able to do so.

The demands of the entitled young adult will look more reasonable than they did coming from your teenager. She will demonstrate a little more patience, and be more artful in her approach. You won't hear her complaining that "everyone else gets to" anymore, because even she knows that's not true. She will learn to make sure that what she wants is positioned as a "need." It's even better if she can get you to think that it's in your best interest as well. For example, if she wants you to give her a down payment and co-sign for a car, she will likely argue that she has no money for a car, and without a car she can't get a job, and without a job she will have to stay at home and continue to rely on you for support. She may even take a nonchalant approach, knowing that if she asks often enough you will eventually give in.

If you are just now recognizing your child's entitled behavior when she is an adult, it can be particularly difficult to accept. You haven't seen or wanted to see it coming, and are now confronted with the reality of an adult child who acts more like a minor child. You are now left with a sense that your child really can't be successful without your help and support. With power and authority come responsibilities and consequences. An adult entitled child has not learned that life is not an à la carte menu. They can't have all the fun and not have to pay the bill, although they might be able to delay it a little. They now have a lot of power and can quickly get into trouble financially and in relationships, have children of their own, self-medicate with drugs or alcohol to ease their frustrations and

41

generally make choices based on the moment with no regard for future consequences.

You may be surprised, at this stage, if you are feeling angrier and more frustrated than in the past. As a loving parent, you were very motivated to protect and provide for you minor child. However, you may have thought that in the same way she grew out of diapers and blankies, she would eventually grow out of her dependence on you and be able to handle her own affairs. Her poor behavior was tolerated because you thought it would end once she reached maturity. Now she's physically bigger than you – and yet you may be wondering if she will ever take responsibility without using you as a crutch or if she's even capable of success. That's pretty scary.

Regardless of How Old Your Entitled Child Is...

You probably know that you have been too soft, a pushover, perhaps even spineless. You may have held your ground here and there, engaged in shouting matches or grounded her from her cell phone for a day, but you haven't been consistent. It hasn't been too difficult for your child to get what she wants without too much being asked of her in return. The road from pampered to enchanting will not be easy for either of you, but you must love her enough to take that path.

This is about you, and if you are ready to put on your big parent pants and take your power back, then you and your child will ultimately benefit. Why ultimately? Because it's likely to get worse before it gets better. Be prepared. If there was ever a time to feel strong and determined as a parent, the time is now. Tap into the pain, the strained relationship between you and your child, her ill-preparedness for what life is throwing at her and how unhappy you both are to gather the resolve you will need.

There is some good news here, which will come in handy when you commit to the changes that will ultimately cure entitled behaviors: she grew up in a loving home and, though entitled, has some wonderful traits and skills that round her out as a person. By pulling back and allowing her to fail or succeed on her own, you will help her to gain confidence in her own abilities and learn what you already know – that self-reliance is always better than a handout.

3

Dealing with the "Old Baggage"

My personal baggage illustrates two extreme ends of the entitlement scale, and fueled my passion for helping others with this issue.

My parents did not spoil me, not even a little. Born at the tail end of The Great Depression, my parents were both impacted by a severe economic environment that required thrift and modesty and punished overindulgence and excess. They were both raised in strict religious families, and had parents that divorced. I was the second of their three children and the only girl. Even in hindsight, my parents were extremely strict. As a child, I felt like they ran a dictatorship. While I knew they loved me, I often felt unloved – or, more accurately, unlovable. Rules were valued above all else, including fun and bonding, and especially silliness.

I woke up on the morning of my sixteenth birthday feeling like the day was my genie and I could have any wish granted. My parents would now allow me to date boys, and within hours I would be the proud owner of a driver's license. I was intoxicated by the possibilities. Without a car and a good prospect for a boyfriend, I had a lot of work to do; but those realities did nothing to curb my enthusiasm.

After my shower I went into the kitchen and was greeted by my mother, who explained how tired she was and that she didn't have the energy to make me a birthday cake. With that statement, my mom forced the genie back into the bottle, leaving me to make the best of the day on my own. I ended up having chocolate cake with my best friend's family, who laughed with me at my horrible driver's license photo and gave me a bikini to help with my boyfriend-acquisition campaign.

My parents provided my brothers and I with the basic necessities, disciplined us with a firm hand and supervised us closely. We were not afraid of them, but we knew better than to cross them or break any rules, and we certainly knew that they were in charge.

My older brother and I responded to our parents' authoritarian discipline by conforming. My older brother was a strict conformist; I was a little more adventurous and managed to stay out of major trouble by not getting caught very often. My younger brother, Wayne, was a rebel. He railed openly against our parents and started making bad choices while still a young teen. His death at the age of forty-one was attributable in part to his failure to take care of himself, and the years he abused his body with alcohol. Both my parents feel that they failed my younger brother.

My parents are now raising my youngest brother's child, Cole. Cole began living with them when he was four, and is now thirteen years old. They have taken the polar opposite approach to parenting with him, lavishing him with toys, electronics and shopping sprees and feeding him only the few foods he likes to eat. Unlike my brothers and me, Cole knows that his grandparents are not in charge.

During a family vacation this summer, Cole complained about the food that was being prepared for dinner and wanted an alternate meal prepared to his liking. Since his grandparents were not in the room, I let him know that was not going to happen and that he could speak to his grandparents about it when they returned. I wasn't surprised by his behavior, but I was surprised when he stood up and proudly announced that he is spoiled and that's why he gets what he wants.

It seems incomprehensible that my nephew is being spoiled – to an extreme – by the same people who were once so strict with my brothers and me. They obviously know how to be disciplined parents; they have done it. They have also acknowledged that they are spoiling Cole, that his entitled behavior is obnoxious, and that they fear it will limit his chances for success as an adult; yet they choose to continue spoiling him anyway. Both my parents are concerned about his behavior, but only my mother is willing to look at alternate solutions. My father, in particular, has decided that strict discipline was the cause of their son Wayne's rebellion, and he is determined not to make the same mistake with his grandson. He is unable to see that he has taken positions on the extreme ends of the pendulum swing, and that in doing so he is ignoring the balanced solutions that lie in between. The reason my parents are spoiling their grandchild is about their personal baggage, not about what's best for Cole.

My father is a perfect example of why baggage is so damaging. He is clearly troubled and burdened by his decision to strictly discipline my brother, and has made a reactive decision to parent Cole differently. He knows that spoiling his grandson is creating new burdens, the price for which Cole will have to pay on his own as he enters adulthood unprepared to take responsibility for himself. Even though my father knows that what he is doing isn't the best for

Cole, he is unwilling to change and risk being too strict. People who are heavily burdened by their own pain and guilt tend to be more reactive than deliberate when making choices.

Steven Covey addresses the importance of reactive versus deliberate decision-making in the first of his "seven habits of highly effective people." He says that our power to choose lies between stimulus and response. Giving up that power and skipping to the reaction means that you are leaving your life decisions to external factors and failing to take responsibility for creating the outcomes you desire.[5] Emotionally charged and painful stimuli simply make it more difficult to be deliberate rather than reactive; they don't make it impossible. If you believe you have deep wounds that trigger strong reactions, you may need to work with a trained mental health professional before you can move from spoiler to disciplined parent.

If you are dealing with your own baggage, you are likely to feel stuck. You may be like my father, who knows that spoiling his grandchild is not in the child's best interest but feels unable or unwilling to change. This creates a whole new level of pain, because you have a sense you could do better for your child if you only knew how. Start with the baggage, because if you do not deal with it, you will stay focused on it and therefore be unable to focus on what's best for your child.

Emotional Baggage from Childhood

All of us, even those of us who had an ideal upbringing, have baggage from our childhood experiences. If it is significant and we haven't dealt with it, it becomes damaging baggage that interferes

---

[5] Steven R. Covey, *The 7 Habits of Highly Effective People* (New York: Free Press, a division of Simon & Schuster, Inc., 1989), 65-94.

with effective decision-making. If there were no obvious traumas in your childhood, it can be tempting to dismiss the possibility that you have any baggage; but that may not be true.

Even if you grew up with an intact family, a stay-at-home mom, well-adjusted siblings and a family dog, you can still have baggage that needs to be addressed. In this circumstance, you may not have seen much conflict; this may have led you to conclude that relationships are easy, or to expect perfection in your own relationships. If you expect relationships and children to be perfect, you may have a low tolerance for mistakes or misbehavior. This could result in parenting from an extreme – as a strict and severe disciplinarian, or as the overprotective mom bent on preventing problems before they occur.

More traumatic events, such as poverty, abuse, neglect, divorce and bullying, have great potential to create emotional baggage. Children are less capable of interpreting what happens to them than adults are, and often create myths or "personal truths" around these events in an effort to make sense of them. These myths remain incredibly powerful because they assisted with coping and survival. They are familiar and comfortable – and the source of emotional baggage.

Were you raised as an entitled child? If so, your pain is potentially doubled. Your parents made things easy for you as a child, but your adjustment to adult responsibilities was or still is difficult. If you have a child, you may be raising him using your parents as role models. You know what entitlement cost you, and now you have sentenced your child to the same.

What Does Baggage Do?

Emotional baggage generally originates in childhood; but unless we put it down, we carry it and the effects of guilt, fear and regret into adulthood. These are three very powerful, negative emotions; and if we feel them, we will either consciously or unconsciously take action in an effort to make them go away.

1) Guilt: You know you did something wrong and feel bad about it.

2) Regret: You know after the fact that you could have done better, and feel bad that you didn't.

   a) Guilt and regret are often grouped together, as the "guilt" parents feel is often really regret, or the wish that they'd had the power to change circumstances.

3) Fear: You are so motivated to avoid what you fear that you are less able to make reasoned decisions.

If you have said any of the following, it may be a sign that you are feeling guilt or regret:

1) My child will never recover from the effects of my divorce

2) I don't get to spend enough time with him

3) I have made a lot of mistakes that have hurt him

4) I have been too selfish, focusing on my needs instead of his

5) I know spoiling him is not in his best interest, but I don't know what else to do

If these questions are haunting you, fear may be your primary emotion:

1) What if he can't succeed on his own because I haven't taught him well?
2) What if I let him do it his way and he gets hurt?
3) What if he gets mad at me?
4) What if he stops loving me?
5) What if he really has a difficult personality and I can't fix that for him?

Guilt, regret and fear are ugly monsters that can be difficult for many to conquer. You may feel guilty about how you have treated your child in the past, how his entitled behavior is negatively affecting him today, or how he is not a successful and thriving adult. Maybe he suffered a trauma as a child and you overreacted to it by attempting to shelter him from any further disappointment or pain. Or maybe you had very little as a child and went overboard with your own child because of what you felt you missed out on. Or maybe you are a single parent with a job and three kids and you feel you were too exhausted and time-challenged to discipline effectively. Take a moment to search for any guilt you might be experiencing and write it down. Often, we gain power over our demons when we expose them to the light of day.

For example, one of the most powerful fears is, "He won't love me anymore if I don't give him what he wants." Few parents speak these words out loud in polite company, but many have this fear and it drives them to overindulge their children in the hope of buying love. In truth, the exact opposite happens; the fear is completely unfounded. Less than half of overindulged children report as adults that they felt loved.[6] Conversely, many children who were not given a wealth of extras, either because their parents did not feel it was appropriate or because they couldn't afford it, did feel loved. Saying no or applying reasonable discipline does not mean that your child won't love you, although he may say it and may even mean it at the time.

Guilt takes up a lot of emotional time and energy that can be better spent elsewhere. You don't want to pretend the past didn't happen, but it's not productive to relive the past repeatedly in your head or let guilt influence your actions in the present. If you feel guilty, you need to acknowledge it, make amends and ask for forgiveness if necessary, and then get on with the business of living.

Freedom of Choice

You must make a conscious decision to parent differently than your own parents did. Otherwise, you will react and repeat the mistakes of the past, or overcorrect and do the exact opposite.

My mother was a yeller when I was growing up. She would yell at what I thought to be slight provocation and sometimes carry on for a while. Many people who experience this go on to yell at their own children. I have talked to friends who realize it and hate it, but yell nonetheless. I crave peace in my home, and decided early on that I would not yell. I have raised my voice at my children on occasion over the years, but it's usually for effect – when I need them to understand that a major event just happened and they had

---

6 David Bredehoft, Sheryll Mennicke, Alisa Potter and Jean Illsley Clarke, "Perceptions attributed by adults to parental overindulgence during childhood," *Journal of Family and Consumer Sciences Education*, vol. 16, no. 2 (Fall/Winter 1998): 12.

better pay attention, like if they broke curfew or lied to me. Both the yellers and the non-yellers are imprinted by their own yelling parents and have had different responses to it.

You can't look at how your parents raised you, label it good or bad, and then set out to repeat it or do the opposite as a knee-jerk response without going overboard or being reactive. I'm not afraid to raise my voice if necessary to make a point, so I don't label all yelling as bad, or feel the associated guilt and shame if I do yell. However, I have also decided that I don't want to follow my mother's example. Instead, I choose to create a calmer environment for my children. This has created a guilt-free and healthy space for me. I have yelled a time or two out of anger or in the heat of the moment, but it hasn't crippled me. I apologize, hug and kiss, and move on.

Put the Baggage Down

Take a moment to grieve, if you haven't done that already. You have made some mistakes that have cost your child some happiness. You haven't robbed him of everything, and there's still time to make changes that will improve the situation; but this isn't what you wanted for him. Grieve for what your mistakes have cost your child. He may still be young and having difficulty with friends or dealing with a low frustration tolerance, or he may now be an adult who is unable to form lasting relationships or be financially responsible. Grieve also for what this has done to your relationship with him. You often feel angry, disappointed, frustrated and sad. This child has great potential, but seems to be tossing it away because he isn't putting forth any effort and is no fun to be around. Take the time to acknowledge the pain, because you will need awareness of it to help remind you why you need to make a change. If you get stuck at this stage and feel that you need help to move on, please take the time to do that, too. To be able to rock your entitled child's world enough to make positive and lasting changes, you need to think clearly and feel empowered.

Take a moment, also, to address the guilt or regret you will likely be feeling. You may be thinking, "Had I been a better mother, he would not be so unsuccessful and lonely (or fill-in-the blank with your child's struggle)." You can't change the past, but you still have today and you can't let guilt hold you back from making tough decisions that can help him moving forward. Remember that you also did many things right, and he has other qualities that you can celebrate. Don't use the good to rationalize the bad, but don't forget or minimize it either.

Liz's Story

A dear friend of mine was spoiled by her parents and then went on to do the same thing to her daughter. I share her story here, along with its positive and hopeful developments, to provide encouragement for those also struggling with entitlement, be it as children, parents, or both. Whether we intend to or not, many of us will either repeat the mistakes of our parents or embrace the exact opposite in response to our baggage.

Liz knows that she was overindulged as a child. Her father traveled extensively on business and showered her with gifts each time he returned home. She cannot remember being denied anything she asked for, and remembers feeling very protected and taken care of.

As she grew older, Liz started to become aware that there might be a cost attached to being spoiled. She began to realize that being taken care of felt great, but unless she wanted to live at home as an adult, she would need to figure out how to take care of herself. The thought terrified her, and ultimately she ended up marrying an older man on whom she could depend. Fortunately, he is a kind and stable person, but as Liz has continued to work toward becoming more self-reliant and exerting her independence, they have had to make adjustments in their marriage.

What Liz has now realized is that she has done the same thing to her daughter Amanda that her father did to her. Knowing the cost of entitlement, she had intentions as a new mother not to spoil her daughter; but ultimately, she made many of the same mistakes. She had inklings that she was being too indulgent and permissive, and her husband complained occasionally that she was spoiling their daughter, but she was unwilling to address it until recently. She still has five years before Amanda graduates from high school to prepare her for self-reliance, and is determined to make major changes. Liz no longer buys her daughter everything she wants. They now have a budget, and they stick to it. Amanda is required to save up for something she wants, or, due to other priorities, she has to go without. Liz is also involving Amanda in charitable causes, working alongside her to help others less fortunate. Amanda was not initially happy with the changes her mom was making, and made a huge fuss at times. And in the beginning, Liz was afraid of upsetting her daughter and feared that Amanda would not love her anymore. As Liz and her husband continue with the changes, supporting each other, Amanda's behavior has calmed down. She is now much more delightful than before.

Liz is happy with the success she is experiencing with her daughter, but is still struggling with her relationship with her father and her own adjustment in overcoming entitlement. She has a great deal of support and determination, and will hopefully continue to make good progress.

It doesn't take an entitled child to raise one. You may have had fabulous parents who served as wonderful parenting role models, or you may have been neglected and self-taught. Either way, you have bought into the myth that your child needs it better, easier and more wonderful than you had it. In giving him "better," you have lost sight, whether completely or just little bit, of what better really is. It's not what you give your child; it's what you teach him about earning his own way.

4

How Did We Get Here?

It is seldom easy to see the end at the beginning of an adventure, especially the adventure of parenting. As you begin to consider that you are raising or have raised an entitled child, you are probably wondering, "How exactly did this happen? When did this behavior start?" You didn't intend to raise an entitled child. You may have wanted to give everything to your child so that she felt loved and cared for, and this may have gone further than you envisioned. Perhaps you didn't anticipate the negative behaviors that are part of the entitlement package. Your intentions were good and you think that she is generally a well-behaved kid, but this entitled behavior has to change.

The question is: How did we get on the road to entitled behavior? This direction began with the first choices you made, and will continue until you make different choices. Let's take another look at my client Jack, whom I introduced in Chapter 1.

Jack is a protective and loving father of three girls. The request for $25,000 for preschool tuition shocked him because it was the first time that he found one of his daughter's requests outrageous. As he told me his story, it was easy for me to see the pattern of a spoiler parent. Jack and his wife are the kind of parents who want everything for their children. He and his wife made sacrifices to make sure that their daughters enjoyed the extras. The daughter asking for the preschool tuition is their middle child, Karen.

Karen was always out of allowance when it was time to go to the movies with her friends. As a younger child, Karen was the one who was impossible to please with food or clothes. She was always demanding, but in such a sweet way that Jack had never found a reason to discipline her. Karen was always able to position her wants as needs and rarely had trouble getting her way. The demands started out small when she was a toddler and grew with her size. Somehow, she managed to not step over the line between reasonable and outrageous with her father for twenty-eight years.

Jack's road to entitlement with Karen is a very common one. Many of us are looking for the obnoxious behavior, and in so doing often miss the less obvious signs. Entitled behavior isn't created overnight. It is a progression that results from a failure to understand that your job as a parent is not to make your child happy, but to teach her how to be responsible, take care of herself and, ultimately, make herself happy.

Think back to when she was born. She literally could not have survived without you. It was your job to provide her with her every need, and sometimes that was a great sacrifice – remember the sleep deprivation? Because of the great love you have for your child, it is natural to want her to be happy and to feel secure, loved and nurtured. The good news is that you can respond every time your infant cries without the running the risk of overindulging her. Many pediatric experts advise that you can't possibly spoil a child at this age. Dr. T. Berry Brazelton agrees that it is impossible to spoil a child younger than twelve months old. Crying is her way of communicating that she needs something, and you simply make her feel secure and improve your bond with her by responding.[7]

After the first year of her life, your child will begin to explore and become more independent. She will still see her world strictly in terms of needs – she wants what she wants. However, it is no longer as simple as it was when she was a baby. She will begin to want things that are not healthy or good for her. For example, she may want to snack on crackers all day, stick objects in an electrical outlet or run out the front door unsupervised. Here's where it begins to get a little tricky. A toddler sees a want and a need as the same thing, and wants you to give her what she's asking for. If you don't, she expects that crying and fussing will give her what she wants because up until now, it always has. She isn't going to know the difference between a want and a need, or how to respond when you deny her what she's after.

Here's the tough part: you can't give in, and you have to teach her the difference. You are looking at her cute face and you don't want her to be unhappy, but you need to help her through his frustration without caving in. If you give in, or if you are inconsistent, you will place your child firmly on the path to entitlement.

Whether you give in often or only occasionally, you may have lost sight of the goal of raising a child, which is preparation for responsible adulthood. If your goal is in the moment – make her happy, stop the whining, stop her arguing – you will be making decisions that trade temporary peace and quiet for her chances at long-term happiness.

Many parents are more lenient with younger children, thinking

---

[7] Dr. T. Berry Brazelton, *Touchpoint Birth to Three: Your Child's Emotional and Behavioral Development* (New York: Perseus Publishing, 1992).

they can toughen up on them once they are older. Responsible adulthood seems a long way away for a really long time. Even during the teen years, it's hard to imagine your child as a rent-paying, voting, making-her-own-meals member of society. She has always been and always will be your baby, but if you treat her that way she'll behave like one long after it's cute and likely to get her what she wants.

If the period from zero to eighteen years is a continuum that begins with complete dependence at infancy and progresses in a straight line to complete independence at adulthood, it's easy to see that a child needs to progress, build skills and gather experience to be able to handle the responsibilities that will be thrust upon her. She will get to age eighteen, but will she have progressed on the zero to eighteen scale of responsibility in equal measure? If you made it easy for her to cruise at a five on the continuum and she's now eighteen years old, she's entitled and unprepared. You did not do her a favor, and the world is going to seem unkind and scary to her. She isn't going to be protected and overindulged for eighteen years and then blossom overnight into a responsible and delightful adult just because she hit that magic birthday.

Why Didn't I See This Coming?

When you're thinking about where you may have gone wrong, you may be thinking of someone else's entitled child. You would never have made those mistakes. You would never have purchased $200 jeans, let her stay out after midnight while still in middle school, or have given her a brand-new sports car for her sixteenth birthday. You have a picture in your head about what type of parenting creates an entitled child and that wasn't you.

59

However, one picture does not fit all. There are more paths to entitlement than you may have considered.

Cloudy Vision

It's very easy to pick out the misbehaving brat across the room at the little-me gym class, but much harder to see the same behavior in your own child and recognize it for what it is. The misbehaving child has thrown himself on the floor at the end of class and refuses to cooperate because he would rather keep playing than go home. You don't live with that child every day or have any love attachment to him, so you see the naughty behavior in isolation and recognize it clearly.

In a cloudy-vision state, the picture looks very different. You know that your child does not always behave like that because you see all the wonderful and enchanting parts of her. You also know that she's had too much sugar today, that this class crowded her nap schedule, and she's been having a rough time adjusting to her new baby brother. In your cloudy vision state, you are more likely to plead with your daughter to stop her temper tantrum, to console her, to cajole her into being more cooperative, and finally to bribe her. You are loaded down with a diaper bag and baby seat with her brother in it, and you're too overburdened and harried to make a stand anyway. You have lowered your expectations for your daughter, and she gets the message. You have also given her your power and, like the four year-old kicking the back of the airplane seat in Chapter 2, she gets that message.

You must be able to feel your parent power and clear your vision in order to help your child with the discipline that she needs to grow and develop. Bad behavior does not mean she's a bad child. You don't need to try to justify or explain away her misdeeds. Of course she is going to act up; that is how she tests her limits and learns valuable lessons. Perfect behavior is not the goal. What is vital to her long-term happiness is helping her learn to expect and predict the consequences of her actions. That will help her moderate her own behavior as she matures. She doesn't need you to force her to behave or be harsh or judgmental if she doesn't. She needs you to teach her how to make good choices and how to behave in such a way that she will get the positive results that she wants in the longterm.

But to do that, you have to recognize her bad behavior without justifying it or explaining it away. When she misbehaves, you must recognize it, handle it effectively, kiss her and move on.

The Many Faces of Entitlement

The second reason you may be struggling to understand how you got to entitled behavior is that three major parenting mistakes set the stage for entitled behavior, only one of which is typically recognized as spoiler parenting. They are neglect, overindulgence and overprotection. How could parenting from two extreme ends of the spectrum – neglect and overindulgence – produce the same result? Because in both cases, the parents give their power away to the child. Okay, then how does overprotection come into play?

Here the child is clearly cherished, and this parent hasn't given any power away. In this case, the problem is one of insulation. This child has been shielded from frustration, disappointment and pain. She has been taught that she is entitled to be cared for. Most parents, even those who do it, are aware that overindulgence will spoil a child. It's the other two kinds of parents, the neglectful and the overprotective ones, who are more often surprised to learn that their child may have an entitlement issue.

Neglectful parents are typically neglectful by default. For them, neglect is an act of omission. The major influencing factors are high-powered careers, more children than resources, single parenthood, substance abuse or simple laziness. The neglected child has been left to cope on her own. Her parent is distracted or absent, leaving a vacuum in which the balance of power falls to the child. Power not earned is not respected. She has the power because no one else has claimed it. She can get what she wants because no one will tell her "no."

The overprotective parent is the least likely to see himself as the spoiler. How can being involved and plugged-in possibly be bad? It's a matter of extremes. This parent hasn't allowed the child any autonomy. So this child expects to be told what to do, which works until she's out on her own. As she begins to experiment in the adult world, she finds that no one is catering to her or fixing all her problems for her. She doesn't know how to cope with frustration or disappointment because she's never had to. She expects life to be easy and for all people to cater to her needs.

Every Child is Unique

The third reason that you may be struggling to understand how you created an entitled child is that every child is unique. It's very difficult for a parent who has successfully raised one or more responsible children to recognize that a younger child may be entitled. Every child has his or her own temperament. What worked with the first child may not have worked with the others. You may have become more relaxed or complacent with this child without realizing it. You could have given all your children too much power or sheltered them all excessively, with varying results. We will discuss this topic in more detail in Chapter 6.

What Do We Do When She's an Adult?

Now your child is not really a child anymore. This day always seemed to live in the very distant future. You aren't even sure you got the hang of parenting a minor child, and now you have to figure out how to be a good parent to an adult child. Isn't this where you just get to be really good friends?

No. You're still her mom or dad, and she will need unconditional love from you for life. And if you were a spoiler, you still represent the gravy train. She's led a very comfortable life, and she will see no reason for that to stop. She won't have the skills to provide for herself in the manner she has become accustomed to while living in your home; but as long as you are still covering for her, she doesn't need them.

And what if your child is still young and you worry about a day when she won't need you anymore? I remember talking with a friend after we had both recently experienced the trauma of a first child leaving home and going off to college. We thought back to the days when it seemed like it would be nice to be a little less needed. With small kids, there were always mouths to be fed, laundry to fold and a surface or body part to clean. And now, after just a couple of weeks, our daughters were having a great time at college. They were making new friends, busy with classes and calling less frequently. The bad and good news was that they didn't need us!

Obviously, your child will always be your child and you will always need each other because of that bond; but the dependency

63

will go away. That's what you have worked so hard for, so don't let it make you feel uncomfortable. It's good that she's so strong and self-sufficient that she doesn't require your help to thrive and be happy.

5

My Circumstances Are Different

Now that you can identify the characteristics of a spoiler parent, the behaviors of an entitled child and how you became a spoiler parent, and you are willing to deal with the baggage, you can get started with solutions.

The first step is to truly understand your unique circumstances. Every family situation is different; however, some families have more challenges than others. This will have an impact on your path to disciplined parenting. Some challenges will resolve over time, and others are unsolvable and need to be managed. That doesn't mean your path to disciplined parenting is blocked – it just means that you will need extra tools or resources. This chapter addresses unique parenting challenges; the following chapter covers the kids' challenges.

Common Challenges

1) You and the other parent or caregiver disagree on discipline – no united front

2) You are divorced and you disagree with your ex-spouse on parenting

3) You are a grandparent with a spoiled grandchild living in your home

4) You have limited resources due to single parenting, a demanding career or other challenges that demand more of your time or energy

5) You are not confident in your own parenting skills, or feel like you will not be able to stand up to your child when he's unhappy or angry

No United Front

The first challenge to solve is providing a united front. If there is more than one parental figure in your child's life, you must be clear and determined together. This includes grandparents living with a grandchild, whether or not the grandchild's parent or parents are also living in the house. You will reinforce the entitled behavior if one of you starts to make changes and the other swoops in to save the poor baby from his mean parent. The marriage or adult relationship may not survive this kind of assault, and that would add to the tragedy.

If not all of the adults in the room are united, your child has an easy way to shift the focus back to you. For example, let's say your sixteen year-old son asks for permission to stay out two hours past normal curfew to attend his best friend's birthday party. You know the details of the party and the other people involved, and you are worried with good reason that the party will turn into an unsupervised drunk-fest, so you say no. Your spouse feels you are being too harsh and robbing your child of a special experience, and says so in front of your child. The two of you begin to argue about how harsh you are and what a softie he is. Meanwhile, your son grabs the car keys and drives to the party. Now you are faced with having to chase him down or letting it go "just this once" – again.

You not only need to stay united, you must not undermine each other. If your spouse feels you are being too harsh but agrees in front of your son that he does not have permission to attend the party, your spouse will inflict even more damage if he says something like, "I agree with you, but your mother always wins." It's fine to disagree, but your child should never know. Disagreements need to be resolved privately, behind closed doors. Otherwise you will undermine each other, and that always leads to disaster. If your child knows you don't trust his other parent's judgment, why should he? And if you argue in front of him you give him ammunition to fight future battles, because he will have gleaned strategic information he can use to strike even harder next time. If he knows that being accused of being harsh is your soft spot, he'll hit you there hard and fast the next time he wants something.

You can't be caught off-guard if you have a game plan prepared ahead of time. Whatever strategy you decide works for your family, make sure that all caregivers agree and that you are committed to supporting each other in front of the child. If you need a coach or referee to help you with a plan both spouses can support and be comfortable with, that's fine. A competent marriage counselor, family therapist or clergy member can assist you with identifying your values and priorities and coming up with a parenting approach that will support your efforts. The exact technique that you use isn't as important as using it consistently and with confidence.

The good news is that stopping the manipulation of one parent against the other in its tracks can be very simple. In my house, we just slowed down the process. When I got a request followed by,

"Dad said I could," I always double-checked with Dad. After being caught trying to play us against each other a few times, my children quickly learned two important lessons. The first lesson was that attempting to manipulate us was never going to work. The second lesson was that they could get more from us by being honest and mature than through lying and manipulation. Once your child understands that divide and conquer will not work for him as a strategy, he won't try it anymore.

Divorce and the United Front

Children are masters at playing one parent against the other. It must be in our DNA. If there's a divorce and stepparents are involved, it's even easier for the child to play the adults against each other because of the communication breakdowns and emotions involved.

Let's face it, you aren't married to your child's other parent anymore because you couldn't resolve your differences, regardless of whether or not they had anything to do with parenting styles. It's crucial for your child that you set your differences aside and make a commitment to work with your ex-spouse to raise your child together (provided you are both fit and willing to participate).

I was divorced from my oldest two children's father when we were only twenty-three years old and the kids were one and three. Babies, all of us. My ex and I were struggling with many issues, including how to effectively co-parent our two children, when a counselor suggested we read Isolina Ricci's, *Mom's House, Dad's*

House: Making Two Homes for Your Child.[8] Ms. Ricci's book, considered by many to be the co-parenting bible, has been updated, and there is now an edition written for children. What still sticks with me today is how critical it is to your child's well-being to make sure both homes are safe and secure. It is equally important that children have parents who are at peace with each other. Getting good advice and help to understand how kids are impacted by divorce is critically important to parenting effectively through this transition. If you, your ex-spouse or both of you have been spoiler parents, and both of you have decided that it needs to stop, you will have challenges your non-divorced peers do not. Your child has some advantages when it comes to resisting your changes, such as the lack of his parents' proximity to and communication with each other, that children in two-parent households don't have. Your game plan to present a united front to your child needs to be even more detailed. You need to have a plan for communication that is consistent, and make sure other parent figures such as stepparents are involved and cooperative.

If you are not in agreement that the spoiler parenting needs to stop, or your ex-spouse is behaving like a "Disneyland parent," you are likely to feel resentful. It would be great to just hang with your child without regard for chores, homework and discipline, but you realize that both of you checking out as parents will only increase his long-term suffering.

It will be more difficult to un-spoil your child if his other parent isn't committed to change, because you will only be able to influence your child's behavior in your house – but it can be done.

---

[8] Isolina Ricci, *Mom's House, Dad's House: Making Two Homes for Your Child* (New York: Fireside, a division of Simon & Schuster, Inc., 1980).

Your child will naturally prefer the free-range parenting style at the other home, and he will often act up and be disrespectful when transitioning back to your home. Your strategy needs to include transition time for him when he comes back from time with his other parent, and structure so that he knows what's expected of him in your house. Your only response to "That's not how we do it at Dad's" is, "You're not at Dad's house now. My rules apply when you are here with me." While your child may think that getting everything he wants is preferable, the structure in your home will make him feel more secure and confident, which is what will make him happy over the long-term.

If you are not a united front with your ex-spouse, it's even more important that your child knows that it's okay for him to love and be loyal to both parents. He will see your differences because they are glaring, and he needs to know that doesn't make one parent "bad" or "wrong." Here are some tips that can help:

1) Recognize differences with your child. Pretending that you are a united front when it's clear you are not will only undermine his confidence in both of you. "Yes, we do it differently," is much better than "Oh, I hadn't noticed," or "I don't like the way Dad does it, but there's nothing I can do."

2) Your house, your rules. While it will be harder for a child who is spending significant amounts of time in homes with completely opposite rules, it's better to provide him structure and discipline in one home than in neither.

3) Never, ever criticize his other parent. "Yes, that's the way Dad does it, and I do it this way," is all the explanation that is necessary. He will resent you if you bad-mouth his father, and he will feel that he needs to stick up for him. As

frustrating as it may be in the moment, this is a rule that, if broken, will cause even more difficulty than keeping silent about your opinions.

4) Find areas where you do agree with his other parent and make sure that your child is aware that you support each other in those areas.

5) Encourage your child to take personal responsibility whether he is in your home or his dad's. Ultimately, he's going to need to get his work done because it's what's best, not because Mom or Dad requires him to do it. If his father doesn't supervise completion of homework on the school nights your child is with him, your child's grades will suffer. Help him understand that he can do his homework at Dad's even if Dad doesn't make him, and reward him when he does.

If you are a stepparent, you have an equally blessed and cursed role.

It is blessed because of the opportunity for a close relationship that you otherwise would not have had. When my husband and I were married, he chose a close, personal, loving relationship with my three children. My oldest two children were adults when my husband and I met and married, so he is less of a father than a protector, a supporter and an advocate for them. My oldest daughter and son appreciate that they can call him for "guy advice" that is unbiased, uncomplicated and given with love. They don't view him as a father, but definitely know that they can turn to him for help and support. My third child is still young and he and my husband have a traditional step relationship. My child knows that he is loved by his mom and his dad, and that his stepfather chooses to love him that much too.

The role is cursed because you don't carry the clout of a "bio" parent, yet you still have the responsibilities of protecting and caring for the child. All the work, none of the glory.

My husband felt very frustrated after we were married because of this dynamic, but after a short time, we created a step-parenting strategy that works for us. I provide the bulk of the discipline for my son, while my husband plays the supporting role. (Think good cop, bad cop, without the manipulation.) Long after we implemented this strategy, which has been working fabulously in our home, I stumbled upon a Dr. Phil column entitled, "What Role Should a Stepparent Play?" He believes that in most cases, the bio parent needs to provide the discipline, while the stepparent needs to be an adult authority figure that is defined as an ally and supporter.[9] I don't argue with what works, I only wish I had seen this article sooner!

If you are a frustrated stepparent whose spouse is spoiling his child, you are in a tough situation with three potential outcomes. The best-case scenario is that you work with your spouse, who decides to become a disciplined parent you can support. Outside of that, you have the option of making the best of a difficult situation or leaving with your blessings. You can't effect change if your spouse is unwilling to take the lead.

Grandparents Not in a Primary Parenting Role

Grandparents who are living with a grandchild and his parent or

---

[9] Dr. Phil, "What Role Should a Stepparent Play?" Dr. Phil's official Web site, "Parenting" page, "Family First" column, http://www.DrPhil.com/articles/article/243 (accessed February 15, 2012).

parents have a tough job. Even in the best of circumstances, when the parent is engaged and doing a good job of disciplining and nurturing the grandchild, it's hard to strike a balance between not meddling and being adequately involved. If your grandchild is already entitled or well on his way down that path, you are caught between the proverbial rock and a hard place. If you try to step in and provide the discipline, you become the mean one. Even worse, your grandchild will run to the safe haven of his permissive parent and the bad behavior will be reinforced. So now you're the mean grandparent with an even brattier grandchild. If you do nothing, you will be stuck dealing with the bad behavior; which will also put a strain on your relationship with your grandchild.

If your child and grandchild are living with you, your only choice is whether or not to allow the behavior in your home. And by behavior I'm talking about the parent's. Your grandchild is behaving exactly as he has been taught and should not be the focus. You need to be the parent for your child and get clear on what you can support and what you cannot support in your home. You don't have the power to help your grandchild, but you can stop enabling your child and hope that he is willing to put on his big parent pants.

If you are a living in your child's home with a spoiled grandchild, your options are very limited. If you are unable to support your child and cannot be peaceful, you may need to consider other living arrangements.

Limited Resources

Life is not neat and very few situations are straight up. Parenting a child is an act of selflessness, with rewards and penalties meted out liberally (though not in equal measure, for some).

Here are some of unique parenting challenges that fall into the category of limited resources:

1) Single parenthood
2) Raising a large number of children
3) Having multiple children, one or more with special needs
4) One or both parents have a time-consuming career
5) Grandparenthood

If you have additional challenges that impact your ability to stay focused on disciplined parenting, you are more likely to raise an entitled child. In the first three cases, it will more likely be due to neglect or overprotection. In the case of grandparenthood or a high-powered career, overindulgence remains a significant danger. A grandparent thrust into the role of primary caretaker of a grandchild can be particularly vulnerable to the cuteness haze in the younger years, and then be completely overwhelmed in the teenage years when physical strength is hugely in the favor of the teen. Grandparents who worked long hours and missed a great deal with their own children may now be very engaged and involved to the point of overcompensating. Others may be stepping into the primary parenting role out of love, but with health or stamina issues that create the same vacuum of power as neglect does.

You made the decision to parent your grandchild, but you didn't create the world in which that choice was a necessary one to make. It's been a while since you have nurtured young ones, and you are now robbed of the traditional grand relationship that you had envisioned. This relationship with your grandchild can be just as sweet and rewarding, but it won't be traditional and you may need to reach out for extra support. Single parents, parents of large families and parents of special needs children may also need additional support. Many parents have established non-traditional relationships that end up benefiting everyone involved.

A man I admire greatly is a single, never-married father of a three year-old boy who lives with an ex-girlfriend as roommates. She is very supportive of my friend, a fabulous role model for his son, and helps defray household costs. This arrangement is clearly nontraditional, but very supportive both economically and emotionally for my friend and his child. Be fearless in looking for solutions if you are overwhelmed or need support.

Lack of Confidence

Fake it until you make it. Then fake it some more until you have mastered it. Sounds good, but how does that actually work?

The primary reason you lack confidence may possibly be that you are not happy with the current results of your parenting skills. If that's the case, then continuing with the current course of action is going to result in more self-doubt. That's a reason to change, but not a reason to feel confident about the change.

One of the most disturbing statements I have heard was from a mother who has an obese child. This mother suffered from poverty and is determined that her daughter will never want for anything. This has resulted in a ten year-old girl who weighs 190 pounds, cannot participate in any physical activity and is totally socially isolated. This mother, when confronted with the fact that she is feeding her daughter to excess and a potential early death, said, "I don't care if it's not what's best for her, I want her to be happy."

Let that give you confidence, or at least the confidence that you need to change. Your child depends on you. If you don't care, who will? If you can't make a stand, who will? Your child is depending on you. She has unlimited potential and needs you to lead the way. You don't have to be alone. Develop a community. Many people are passionate about children; many of them do not have children of their own. We all benefit when children have the support and resources they need to become healthy, contributing members of society. You are not asking too much when you ask others to help you and your child. If you don't have the confidence to go it alone, have the confidence to move forward with support. When you are at home and your child is angry, call someone. Backing down is going to put you right back where you started. Rallying the troops is going to move you and your child one step forward. You can do one step!

6

My Kid Is Special

Kids are challenging from the start. My youngest son began life by peeing on his nurse. We didn't see that one coming, and his nurse's startled response confirmed that she didn't either. Some babies come into the world screaming and loud while others are quiet, seeming to soak in their new surroundings. Each child brings her unique self to the childrearing equation, and some will be more challenging than others.

As with unique parenting circumstances, special issues your child faces may be presenting you with increased challenges on your path to disciplined parenting. Some challenges will resolve over time, while others are unsolvable and must be managed. This chapter addresses issues associated with healthy children. Help from mental health or medical professionals will be needed for children with more serious emotional or mental health issues.

Here are five examples of unique challenges presented by healthy children developing along a typical path:

1) Each child is unique – a parenting style that worked with one

child may not be working with the next one

2) Your child is defiant or extremely stubborn – she will not cooperate

3) Your child is just like you – sparks fly

4) Your child is the exact opposite of you – what makes this child tick?

5) She is extremely bright or has excessive energy – you can't get her attention or keep her focused for long

Each Child Is Unique

I remember the birth of each of my four children in great detail and with great emotion. I remember the overwhelming joy I felt as each one drew a first breath and claimed a place in the world. Part of that was gratitude for a healthy delivery, but it was also about the endless possibilities each little one represented.

My first child was the smallest and, as it turned out, my only girl. The nurses called her "Miss Priss" because she extended her pinkie finger as if sipping fine tea from a delicate cup. She is eleven inches shorter than her younger brother and will likely be shorter than her twelve and two year-old brothers, once they are fully grown. She's tough and determined, but in a feminine, sensitive way.

My second, my first boy, was the biggest and the quietest baby. He still is the strong-silent type and fiercely protective of the women in his life. At six feet-four inches, I'm glad he's on my side!

My third was very happy in the womb and finally had to be extricated by the doctor. He screamed for the first six months of his life – was he letting me know exactly how he felt about losing his warm and comfortable pre-natal home? He still dislikes change, but is otherwise very happy and content.

My last child was just minutes old when he peed on his nurse. I have a feeling that we have a spirited boy on our hands. He gives new meaning to the "terrible twos." He pinched his father this morning because he didn't want to share hugging me with anyone. He thinks he's ready to run the show all by himself, right now. What doesn't exhaust us will make us stronger!

All children are born with unique temperaments and talents, some of which are apparent almost from the very first hour of life. As a young mother, I remember thinking that all babies must raise their pinkie fingers and want constant cuddling since that's what my first did. My second was not a fan of cuddling and my fourth wouldn't even let us hold his bottle for him after he figured it out for himself at four months. I have children on both ends of the snuggling spectrum. If I snuggled with them all equally, my daughter wouldn't have gotten enough and my son would be pushing me away.

That's the nature side of the equation that says you have what you have at birth. The nurture side of the argument says that you and your child's environment and experiences will influence his personality and characteristics. We know that nature and nurture play very interactive roles in child development, and both are important factors. I have heard nature and nurture used as an excuse for an entitled child's behavior. Both are contributing factors, but neither can be the sole, complete answer. Nature can present a challenge that will require us parents to adjust the nurture side of the equation.

All children present varying degrees of challenge, but if mentally healthy, all should be enchanting and make it to adulthood as grateful, delightful, contributing members of society. We've all heard the phrase, "There are no bad dogs, just bad pet owners." The same can be said for kids and parents. All mentally healthy kids have the potential for a balanced adult life; it's up to us, the parents, to lead them to success. To do that effectively, we need to adjust our parenting style to support and nurture their unique characteristics.

For example, parenting a more cooperative child in the same manner as a more willful child would have very different results. My friend Carol has two boys who are two years apart in age. Her oldest, William, is a calm, sweet child who plays very well with others. He does not challenge her discipline and rarely gets into mischief. He is so easy that she was able to keep her entire china collection on shelves that were within his reach when he was a toddler. Those of us who gathered often at her house for play dates with more active or more persistent toddlers were always on the run, putting barriers or distance between the china and our curious babies.

When Carol's second child Charlie arrived, he was obviously a much stronger personality. Even as an infant, he wanted attention immediately if he was hungry or needed a diaper change. When he started to crawl, he immediately headed for the china collection. After two harrowing weeks and four broken pieces, Carol packed up the china and moved it out of harm's reach.

Carol called me to apologize. She admitted that she had secretly felt I was not disciplining my son well, since he was one of the kids always trying to get to her china when we visited her home. It wasn't until she experienced Charlie's personality that she realized what worked for William would not necessarily work for other children and that I was dealing with a child more like Charlie. She felt awful about being judgmental and wanted advice on how to deal with her younger son.

My oldest two children represent a good example of very

different personalities as well. It was important to me that my children graduate from college, but I also felt they would apply themselves more and be more appreciative if they also contributed financially to a portion of the cost.

My oldest is extremely conscientious, completed her college applications on her own, applied for grants and scholarships and was very cooperative with me when we sat down to plan her budget and discuss how much I was able to contribute. She earned her bachelor's degree in four years from UC Davis with minimal debt and no major bumps along the road. My second child was more lax in his preparation, asked for more assistance than his older sister, and was much less focused during his three years at UCLA. After struggling with grades, he decided to take a break and is now working full-time and paying off his loans. Hopefully, he will go back to finish his degree at a state college in the fall. I love and admire them both, and respect their different paths. However, I made it clear to my son that I wasn't willing to subsidize the failing grades and lack of focus that probably induced his decision to take a break. I'm sure if I had kept paying the bills, he would have continued to enjoy his time at UCLA without getting any closer to graduating. The point is that I didn't tolerate entitled behavior from my children, ever. Regardless, they have very different personalities and temperaments and one decided to test me in a huge way while the other gratefully accepted my help and used it wisely. If I had parented my son the same way I parented my daughter, he could have easily developed entitled behavior.

You may have been lulled by an easy first child and run into the entitlement monster with your second, simply because you parented both the same and that only worked for the one whose personality is more mature. You may not suffer from entitlement, you may have one or more children who are enchanting and responsible, and still you may have raised or may be raising a pampered child.

Your Child Is Defiant

Defiant is defined as boldly resistant or challenging. Some kids are naturally more stubborn and challenging, while others develop defiant behaviors for a variety of reasons, including neglect and abuse. If your child is uncooperative to any degree, she will test you to the ends of your endurance when you begin to un-spoil her.

You are going to need additional tools to parent your extremely uncooperative child. Understanding her behavior, what motivates it and how to best work with her is critical. Dr. Rudolf Dreikurs, an American psychiatrist and educator, is recognized for having developed a method for understanding undesirable behavior in children and stimulating their cooperation through logical consequences without punishment or reward. He believes that all misbehavior is the result of a child's mistaken assumption about the way she can find a place and feel important in her world.[10] In other words, a child will act out because she feels that she doesn't belong, and will attempt to regain control or status by acting out in one of four ways:

1) Attention-seeking

2) Attempting to gain power and control

3) Seeking revenge

[10] *Encyclopaedia Britannica Online*, s.v. "Dreikurs, Rudolf," http://www.britannica.com/EBchecked/topic/171320/Rudolf-Dreikurs (accessed February 15, 2012).

4) Acting helpless

A common example is an out-of-control preschooler who is misbehaving to get the attention she feels she lacks. You have likely experienced this while trying to have a phone conversation punctuated by her repeated interruptions.

Dreikurs and other mental health professionals have developed methods that involve applying logical consequences, without punishment or rewards, to stimulate the child to be responsible for her own good behavior. "Redirecting Children's Behavior" is a class available through the International Network for Children and Families that is strongly influenced by Dreikurs' work. "Parenting with Love and Logic" is a parenting approach that is also centered on teaching parents to discipline using consequences rather than punishment. There are others as well, but regardless of the method you choose, please understand that your child's behavior is not a personal reflection on you. You need to be able to view it from a clinical perspective so that you can approach the solution without anger or irritation, parenting her calmly and with empathy. This can be extremely difficult if the defiant behavior has been going on for a long time, if your child is angry at you and says hurtful things or if you tend to engage your child at her level. When applying a logical consequences approach, it is extremely important that you are also encouraging. Your child needs to know that you believe in her, especially after she has made a mistake. You will be working with her to improve her behavior. It won't be perfect every time, even after you have established a new norm and calmed her defiant behavior. As her behavior improves, you will need to continue to recognize her achievements, focus on her success, and provide ongoing support.

As referenced above, Dreikurs outlined the four types of behaviors engaged in by disruptive children:

Attention Seeking

This child feels like she isn't getting enough attention and recognition. Many parents are surprised to learn that their child falls into this category, because they feel engaged and attentive. If that's the case with you, your child's need is higher than what she's getting, even if you lavish her with attention. It may not be that her need is unusually high; it may be that the type of attention you are giving her isn't the kind that she responds to. For example, some children have a high need for physical touch to satisfy their need for attention. If you are not comfortable with touch, or if your own personal need for it is low, you may be unknowingly starving your child of the attention she craves. Because she isn't getting attention for her positive behaviors through physical touch, she will act out. When she misbehaves and you engage with her, she successfully got your attention but for the wrong reason. If your child is seeking attention by acting out, giving it to her when she acts out plays into her plan and further reinforces the negative behavior. You will need to minimize uncooperative behavior, distract her and recognize appropriate behavior immediately when it does happen. If her behavior becomes disruptive, she needs to be given the choice between continuing the disruptive behavior and having a consequence, or engaging in a more desirable activity. For example, if she is refusing to get ready for bed, you can give her the choice of a time-out if she chooses to be obstinate, or five extra minutes snuggling in bed with a book if she cooperates.

It can be difficult to figure out why your child is engaging in attention-seeking behavior, particularly if you are an involved parent and you spend time with her. If this is the case, it's likely that she's not responding to the type of attention you are providing – which to her is the same as not getting any. I have found Gary Chapman and Ross Campbell's book, *The Five Love Languages of Children*, to be extremely helpful when looking for solutions to this type of problem. If your love language is different from that of your child, you may doing everything you know how to show her that you love and respect her, but she won't hear it.[11] Learning your child's love language and adjusting your approach to her could be what she needs to feel that she belongs.

Attempting to Gain Power and Control

The child acting out in this manner feels inferior. She will attempt to assert power or control over those around her through disruptive or attention-seeking behavior. This child doesn't just want attention; she wants to be the boss so that she improves her feeling of importance. You absolutely cannot engage your child in the battle she creates. Strategies for dealing with this behavior are similar to those for the attention-seeking child.

When dealing with a child attempting to assert control, you must provide her with an excellent role model. You will need to face her challenge with calm and handle her behavior in an adult, responsible manner. She needs to see that a person can be unhappy and frustrated and still act appropriately. For example, a child attempting to gain control may berate and yell at her parent. With an act that shocking, it is easy to react in anger and hurt rather than as a calm,

---

[11] Gary D. Chapman and Ross Campbell, MD, *The Five Love Languages of Children* (Chicago: Northfield Publishing, 1997).

responsible parent. You may need additional support or training to be able to help your child if she is determined to gain power, or keep power if you have given yours away to her.

Seeking Revenge

This child has become discouraged after failing to get attention or gain power over a period of time. She now wants to hurt adults to retaliate for the way she feels she has been hurt. It will be hard to feel affection for this child, but that is exactly what she needs. She will need patience while she learns to recognize that you care for her and to trust that you will continue to care. When she is acting out, do not engage at her level. She needs to be responsible for her actions, and to experience appropriate consequences when she acts up.

Acting Helpless

This child has given up. She has not been successful at getting attention or gaining status or control, and no longer cares what happens. She will need even more patience and support to build her confidence. Focusing on success and providing encouragement will work best with this child. She needs to know that you believe she is capable of appropriate behavior and that you can let her make a mistake. She will only gain confidence and improve her behavior if she believes that you believe in her and support her.

All four of these behaviors – seeking attention, seeking control, seeking revenge and acting helplessly – represent defiance. The challenge of parenting a defiant child is that it often leads to entitlement because you cede power to her by simply engaging. She wins if you join the battle. To be successful in un-spoiling your defiant or extremely stubborn child, you need to be able to identify the type of disruptive behavior she is engaging in from the four areas described above, use logical consequences to stimulate appropriate behavior, provide encouragement and work for improvement, not perfection. You must be sensitive to your own needs as well, and realize that you are facing a big challenge for which you may need additional support.

Your Child Is Just Like You

While you both are wonderful, having a child with the same personality traits as yours often sets the stage for confrontation. For example, if you are both stubborn, epic battles will ensue unless you are able to recognize and temper your own behavior. In doing so, you will teach her to curb her own willfulness. Stubbornness can be a useful skill if used with restraint. Many enormously successful people credit their accomplishments to an unwillingness to consider failure an option. Use your similarities to work together in refining the characteristic that you find yourselves clashing over. For example, if you both have a short temper, you have years of experience dealing with the negative effects of lashing out in anger. If you have already learned to recognize early warning signs, how to de-personalize the situation and how to use calming and coping techniques, you can teach them to your child.

What if the trait you share with your child is one that you are still struggling with and don't like in yourself? You may be experiencing additional distress if your child behaves the same way you do because you feel responsible for that trait. While that isn't true, you may feel at a loss to help your child because you haven't figured out how to cope with your own issues. If this is the case, you'll need outside support to resolve your own problem before you can help your child.

Your Child Is the Exact Opposite of You

This can be just as difficult as having a child just like you, but in different ways. You may truly be mystified about what makes this child tick. This can be problematic because in order to apply consequences and motivate her, you need to understand what is important to her.

When applying logical consequences and encouragement, you need to reach her on her level. Every child has a currency; some may just be more difficult to discover than others. For some, it's quality time spent with you; for others, it's time alone to relax and chill.

My oldest child is my twin, while my second child is my polar opposite. With my oldest, a time-out in her room was very effective. She is a very social creature, and even a couple of minutes alone in her room were enough to correct her behavior. My second child could spend hours alone in his room, happily parking his cars in intricate patterns or reading books, even when he was very young. Putting him in time-out in his room was a treat, something I had to recognize before time-outs began to work for him. It took me a while to figure it out because as a social creature myself, I thought he would naturally want to behave if faced with time alone in his room. When I realized it was a treat for him, we designated a timeout chair in the kitchen where he would have to sit with no distractions until he agreed to cooperate.

If you don't understand how to work with your child, you need to figure her out, and you can enlist support and help from others to do that. You will need to resist the natural tendency to treat your child as you would like to be treated.

She Is Extremely Bright or Has Excessive Energy

I have a dear friend whose eight year-old child's IQ is in the superior intelligence range. He has already failed to thrive in public school because it's too boring and decided that Cub Scouts is for babies, and he often stages intellectual battles with his mother. While his high intelligence is a tremendous gift, it also presents incredible challenges. His mother is also extremely intelligent, but often feels at a loss when trying to direct his unbridled curiosity and enthusiasm. Her disciplinary techniques have been patterned after those described above for defiant children; but he is less defiant than completely sure of his own abilities and is unconvinced of the need to submit to parental authority. He really believes that he can take care of himself and make his own decisions. He obviously cannot, but he doesn't have the maturity or insight at age eight to understand that he doesn't yet know everything.

A child with excessive energy presents similar challenges. If your child has unlimited energy she may feel invincible, and you may require more stamina to parent her effectively.

Both the extremely bright kids and those with excessive energy need to be stimulated and will benefit from the techniques used for defiant children. They need a stronger parental influence because they feel so invincible. The risk of power being transferred from parents to children in these circumstances increases because of their advanced reasoning skills and seemingly unlimited stamina. If your child is excessively bright or energetic, you need to be at the top of your game as a parent!

The Risk of Unique Challenges

Some of the unique personality traits or issues your child is presenting will fall into the category of a good taken to the extreme, such as energy or intelligence. Others will be more innately challenging, such as a short temper. While we often hear that we should observe moderation in all things, we also know that extraordinary achievements are not a result of moderation. We have Benjamin Franklin's famous quote, "Do everything in moderation, including moderation," on the one hand, and Oscar Wilde's "Moderation is a fatal thing. Nothing succeeds like excess," on the other. There will be pros and cons to your child's unique personality. Your challenge is to refine the cons (moderation according to Franklin) and encourage the pros (moderation according to Wilde) while retaining your role as a leader.

Please recognize that when you are fatigued, you are at increased risk for giving your power to your child in the face of unique challenges. Maintaining your perspective and getting assistance where needed will be crucial to working with your unique child to bring out her best and retaining your parental power.

End of Part One

Part Two

What Did I Do Wrong?

7

Parent Power

How do you feel about power?

How do you feel about power and the dynamic it creates between you and your child? The truth is that the power in a parent-child relationship is naturally yours, your child wants it, and if you give it to him he will be unable to use it to his own good.

If you don't want to be a spoiler parent, you need to understand that you have the power in your parent-child relationship. You are older, wiser and more capable, and it's absolutely right and necessary that you have the power. How do you feel about that? What is your gut reaction to the word "power?" Do you naturally shy away, or do you feel filled with purpose and ready to take action? If you don't want to be a spoiler parent, you need to embrace your power and understand that power is amazing and can be used to accomplish great things. You may be uncomfortable with power because it was misused or abused with you in the past. You can do better, and you will need your power to help your entitled child. If you've given too much or all of your power to your child, you are going to have to take it back – and he won't like it or you for a while.

All children want the power, although the degree to which they fight for it can vary greatly. It's what fairy tales and candy-coated dreams are made of. A child will abuse power because he will use it only to satisfy his immediate desires, with no regard for his longterm health, wealth and happiness. He doesn't have the maturity to anticipate the consequences of his actions or to give up momentary happiness for long-term gain.

Power issues are more difficult when it comes to the areas that are completely within a child's control. Toileting and eating both fall into this category. If you are struggling with an issue in either of these areas and it has become a health or safety issue for your child, I would recommend getting help from a family therapist or counselor. If you were inconsistent with your toddler and he will only eat white rice, ketchup and sweets now, you have a serious health problem on your hands. That problem needs to be addressed before there are long-term consequences like diabetes, obesity and dental decay. It could also blossom into an eating disorder. Such disorders carry a high mortality rate and are very hard to treat later in life. Prevention and taking decisive action are clearly preferable to the health problems that will arise later if these issues are not addressed.

Recently I saw a story about a young man living in a college dorm who collapsed and needed emergency medical attention. This was shocking enough. A young and seemingly healthy boy is the last person you would expect to see on a stretcher, loaded into an ambulance and rushed to the hospital. More shocking was the story behind the story. This college freshman had refused to eat anything except pizza from a very young age, and his parents had allowed him to dictate his own diet. Breakfast, lunch, dinner and snacks all consisted of pizza. Because of his poor diet choices, this young man now has the serious medical issues that typically face the elderly. It's probably clear to his parents now that they did him no favors by allowing him to eat only pizza. I'm sure they wish they could go back and change things to alleviate his current suffering.

If your child is like most, he will put up a fuss; but if you have a loving relationship, he can adjust to the new power structure. He will ultimately feel more in control and more loved once he sees that you are calm and in control and appropriate boundaries are in place. I don't know why this young man's parents allowed him to eat pizza exclusively, but it's not hard to imagine that their early attempts to feed him healthier alternatives were met with resistance to which they caved. It's also not hard to imagine that they regret giving him so much power over his diet, and the dire health consequences that have resulted.

As you can see from this story, a mistake parents of entitled children make is that they have given their power in the parent-child relationship to the child.

The next six chapters will focus on the common mistakes parents of entitled children make. These mistakes set a foundation for entitlement that needs to be understood and changed before solutions can be effective. Building solutions on a shaky foundation limits the chance for long-term success, so let's tackle the mistakes first. Following this discussion, the next six chapters will focus on solutions.

How Did You Give Your Power Away?

If your child is entitled, you have given at least some of your power away. How did that happen? Think of the power of a two year-old's temper tantrum. I have seen many over the years, some wimpy ones and some that were impressive. I have also witnessed wimpy and impressive parenting in response, not always equal in scale to the tantrums. In fact, a parent who is addressing tantrums in a calm and effective manner will likely never see a colossal tantrum unless they have a particularly willful and stubborn child. Did you calmly wait through the tantrum and then let your child know that he is not going to get the toy today, and he needs to behave or you will take him home immediately? Or did you try to cajole him or comfort him in an effort to stop the tantrum, and then put the toy in the shopping cart when he started up again? If you put the toy in the cart, you taught him a lesson about power that he will be able to use to get what he wants over and over again.

What are you really teaching your child if you have given your power to him? You have taught him that he can have power that he didn't earn, and if he misuses it, you will rescue him.

By retaining your power as a parent, you show your child how it can be used appropriately. As he develops a healthy respect for power, he will be able to appreciate that it can be used for good and bad. He will understand that power marries privileges with responsibilities, and that he must earn the right to his own power as it is appropriate to his age and maturity level.

Please understand that the transfer of power, once started, is difficult to stop. Your child craves it, and as he gets a taste for it, he will want more. You can't give him some power and expect that he won't fight you for more. Many parents end up completely transferring their power to the child after intentionally giving him just a little. Perhaps your child dislikes going to bed and constantly resists any bedtime routine you have established. You are tired of the battles, and negotiate with him to establish a flexible bedtime that is driven by whether he is tired or not on a given night. This is not an outcome that a powerful parent would agree to, because it puts the child in danger of not getting enough rest. Even worse, your child will know that he has won; and once he gets a taste of being the boss, he'll look for more opportunities to shift the balance of power. You can't give away "just a little" of your power.

A Child Doesn't Understand "Too Much of a Good Thing"

The person who has the power in the parent-child relationship impacts the quality of decisions that are made to support your child's healthy development.

I know many adults who were given every material thing they wanted or needed as kids. Some have gone on to up the ante with their own children out of a well-intentioned desire to make their children's lives even more comfortable. We've all seen this in the highly public lives of heirs and heiresses who are making a complete mess of things after being given an abundance of material things as children. Just as with medicine, if some is good, more is not always better.

In addition to more not always being better, bad is not necessarily bad. Your son thinks vegetables and fruits are bad, but having a diet that includes the nutrients available from living plants is obviously good and necessary. Kid logic says more is better and bad is really bad. You can't let him be the judge of situations in which he lacks sufficient maturity or wisdom to make a good decision. You have to step up and make the decisions for him – which teaches him, over time, to make good choices for himself.

Power Shift When Your Child Is An Adult

You still have power as a parent when your child turns eighteen, although it changes dramatically now that your child is legally responsible for himself. You know that getting enough rest, exercise and nutrition are important to his quality of life, but you have zero control over that now. He may even have learned the lessons you taught him and now chooses to ignore them despite the consequences. For example, many college freshmen make poor choices when prioritizing study habits with social activities and earn failing grades as a result. For many, the temptation to play is too strong, while others feel invincible and convince themselves that they can play and work hard without any ill effects. If you allow your child to suffer the consequences of his choices, you are retaining your power as a parent.

Your power has shifted in a monumental way, because you have moved from primary caretaker to a spot in the supporting cast. You will still be very important to him, but now he'll be finding his own way and looking to others in the supporting cast for guidance as well. You have power because he needs you. You are the only one who will always love him no matter what. This power looks very different, and you might not even recognize it as power. You may feel very helpless, like you can't influence him anymore. But this new power is possibly even more potent than what you had before. You are now free to set the boundaries and continue to love him to pieces no matter what. This is going to feel really good and empowering once you get the hang of it.

So what does it look like in everyday life? Let's say you just found out about the F in biology. If he's on a full-ride scholarship or paying his own way through college, then your role is simply a supportive one. He knows what he's doing that's contributing to his poor grades, he just needs to figure out if his priority is partying or getting his bachelor's degree. He will want to believe that both are possible, and in reality, some kids do manage to have a lot of fun and still graduate.

However, if you are paying all or a portion of the tuition, you can have a conversation about your expectations and consequences. My oldest son was not focused on his education at college, and after a semester it was clear to me that he wasn't getting more serious about his studies. I simply told him that I couldn't pay for the grades he was bringing in because he was capable of much better. Unless he brought his grades up to a C or better, I would not be contributing toward his expenses anymore. He would either need to figure out a way to pay them on his own or take a break and go back to school when he was ready. His next semester was just as bad, so I made good on my promise and stopped sending money. He decided to take out loans and get things turned around. I thought that paying for school would make the difference, but he still did not do well. I wasn't there, so I don't know all the factors that contributed to his lack of success, but what I know for sure is that he is a very bright kid and if he had applied himself he could have easily passed his courses and earned a degree. He just wasn't ready, and was only going to waste his time and my money if I kept enabling him.

In this example, being powerful had nothing to do with the ability to control my child's behavior. I can't do that anymore because he is now an adult. The power has shifted from active to passive. I no longer have the ability to check his homework, make sure he goes to class and set curfew to ensure he gets enough rest. Instead, I have to let him know that I believe in his ability to make good decisions, and that I will not support him financially if he does not. He didn't make the choices that I would have liked, but I have to trust that it will ultimately be the best for him, both in terms of learning a valuable lesson and going back and finishing his degree when he is ready for the responsibility.

You Are in Charge Because You Are More Capable

We don't put those least able to handle a task in charge, nor do we make sure that our instructions are okay with them. What directions are we given in the event of an emergency on an airplane? Let those least able to make good decisions be the first in line to make them? Chat about the options and different ideas on how best to proceed? No! Those who are most capable are to secure their own air masks first and then help those requiring assistance. A strong, responsible adult needs to sit next to the emergency door so that she can yank it open and help others deplane. Our children need us to be in charge, to retain our power and to be disciplined parents, or everyone will pass out from a lack of oxygen.

8

Think Before You Speak

According to the Health and Human Services' National Health Interview Study 2000, by the time adults are forty-five years of age, 84% of males and 86% of females have at least one biological child.[12] This means that most of us, regardless of our ability, skills or enthusiasm for parenthood, have procreated. Few of us have had any training. For many, getting pregnant is relatively easy, and after your child's birth, the only thing a hospital is required to do is make sure you have a car seat in which to transport your under-ten-pound human being home. Nobody is making sure you have the tools and skills you need to raise an emotionally, physically and spiritually healthy child. Initially, we are left to instinct, intuition and patterning after our role models.

One of the biggest barriers to raising an emotionally healthy and unspoiled child is also the most difficult to curb because it is so automatic – the ability to resist reaction in favor of a more reasoned

[12] Tamara Halle, PhD, "Charting Parenthood: A Statistical Portrait of Fathers and Mothers in America," Table 1, United States Department of Health & Human Services official Web site, http://fatherhood.hhs.gov/charting02/index.htm (accessed February 26, 2012).

and well-considered response. Reaction is based on emotion and lacks control. Response is more intellectual and involves a purposeful thought process. The trigger for reaction begins with the stimulus. We know what the stimulus is – the tantrum, emotional outburst or naughty behavior from a child. The question is whether you react or respond. A spoiler parent is typically reacting instead of responding to his child.

Why Does This Happen?

As mentioned in Chapter 3, parents who react have not developed the ability to slow down what happens inside them after a stimulus occurs. If your teenage daughter is yelling at you because you told her she cannot go to a party, emotions are running high. Your daughter really wants to go and will pull out all the stops to increase her chances of being given permission. She doesn't have the maturity to negotiate calmly or accept the fact that you are not going to let her go. She fights, you hold your ground, she resists – and you feel bad and give in. Equally reactive but just as destructive is the scenario in which she resists, you insist, she begins shouting and hurling insults and you get angry and return the screaming attack until one of you storms off.

Reaction is automatic; it often happens before the logical side of your brain has a chance to realize what is happening. On a multiple choice test, it is more likely that parents would select the answer that says, "You should engage your angry child in a calm, responsible manner," versus "Yell right back at her." However, in the heat of the moment, if we haven't learned to slow down the process, we will be more likely to get angry and yell.

There are three circumstances in which you are more likely to react instead of respond:

1) Issues from your own childhood are significant

2) You are currently facing significant personal issues

3) Your child's behavior is extreme

If you are reacting instead of responding, you are unintentionally giving away some of your power, because your child will recognize this as fighting on her level. She has a better chance of winning if you are not behaving as a disciplined parent.

Issues from Your Own Childhood Are Significant

I'll use myself as an example here. As a result of my experience with very strict parents, I wasn't entirely sure that I wanted to have children of my own. Why be driven, frugal, conscientious and successful if I couldn't have any fun or joy along the way? My assumption was that adding children to the equation sucked the life out of the party. Clearly I was wrong.

For many reasons, most of them having to do with my need to be the architect of my own life and to dramatically change its framework, I got married just before I turned nineteen. I was on what was called the "mini-pill." It was called "mini" because it had (almost) all the benefits of the regular birth control pill but with less medicine, and therefore was purported to have fewer side effects. Here's where the "(almost)" comes into play. I was pregnant within a month of my wedding day, and my first child was born exactly ten months after I said, "I do." My original thought of not having children was now out the window. I knew that I didn't want to raise my daughter following the example set by my parents, but beyond that I didn't have much of a plan. Looking back, that may have been exactly what I needed to set the scene for change. Research has shown that it is easier and more likely that we will model our parents' example into adulthood, even when we consciously want to do otherwise. Early modeling is a powerful teacher, and responsible for defining what is familiar. Without an enormous desire to create a life very different from the one I had experienced as a child, I am not sure I would have recognized that I had the power to choose a new path.

Less than five years after my wedding day, I was divorced and raising two very young children on my own. Not all my decisions were the best, but I was dedicated to growing and learning as a person and devoted to my children. Fun and joy are wonderful, but they don't pay the bills or keep the house clean. I recognized that I needed the structure and discipline of my parents' house, but that my spirit would die if I didn't figure out how to make it more enjoyable. Nobody would benefit if I chose the path of a martyr.

In the beginning, I was more reactive and likely to choose fun and flexibility over housework and structure. As I realized that being disciplined did not have to exclude fun, I began to relax and make more thoughtful, less reactive decisions. It was definitely a process, in which I gained confidence as I made better and better decisions.

Another example may help illustrate the point. A friend of mine, Carrie, has a child who is extremely obese – more than sixty pounds overweight at the age of six. Carrie has little insight into why her son is extremely overweight. She claims that she does not overfeed her child and that there must be medical issues contributing to the obesity. Carrie's parents were very poor and worked long hours to provide a meager existence for her and her brothers. Carrie often went to school hungry and went to bed with no dinner. When Carrie had a child, she was determined that her own child would never go without food like she did. Out of pure emotion, she fed her child. And fed her child. She did not view it as overfeeding, but rather keeping her son from going hungry.

Carrie knows her child is overweight and faces significant health risks due to his obesity. However, she cannot imagine her child feeling hunger and refuses to consider any solution that involves fewer calories. In Carrie's words, "I know I'm hurting my son, but I don't care. It's better than going hungry."

Patterning from childhood is powerful because it is familiar, even normal. Breaking negative patterns requires that you recognize them and resolve them by dealing with your own issues around the negative patterns. Only then you can decide to act differently for your child. Carrie knows that experiencing chronic hunger is painful. It is a negative pattern that she does not want her child to repeat. She recognizes it and has decided to act differently, but she skipped the most difficult and important step. She has not dealt with the baggage and resolved the pain from her own childhood. Because she has not resolved her own pain, it is now causing pain for her son.

Let's take a detailed look at the three steps critical to breaking negative patterns left over from childhood: first, recognize; second, resolve and third, act differently.

Recognizing unresolved issues can be difficult for many. What happened to you when you were a child seems normal, making it more difficult to identify underlying negative patterns. You might have a sense that something is not right, but be unable to pinpoint the source. Rely on your spouse, partner, friends or counselor to figure it out. You may have to dig deeply and pick at some scars, but you cannot resolve the issue and do better for your child if you don't take the time to identify the source.

Resolving childhood issues or traumas is the most difficult step. Deep emotional wounds may need to be healed with the help of a counselor. I found that many of my clients had participated in extensive counseling and still felt stuck. I shared with them a process that worked for me, and many of them also found it helpful:

1) Once it is recognized, shine a bright light on the issue. Understand all the factors and people involved, how you felt and what you did in response. Be clear about your own role. You were a child and not responsible for poor circumstances or any abuse or bad behavior directed toward you. Don't rationalize how you felt. If you were poor and hungry and that felt awful, let it feel awful. You won't get past it if you try to minimize it or pretend it was no big deal. You were embarrassed, hungry, and angry at your parents for not providing better. Don't hide from the more difficult feelings, like being angry at your parents. As an adult you might feel that being angry at them is unfair, but this is how you felt as a child.

2) It may be hard to intellectually accept, but the second step is to understand that the person who hurt you did the best they could or what they were capable of at the time. This holds true even for the criminally insane, as they are legally recognized to be incapable of recognizing the nature or wrongfulness of their acts. The person who hurt you may have been abused as a child or raised in an extreme religious environment, have an impulse-control or anger problem or be terribly misguided. Whatever the circumstances of the person who hurt you, from the extreme of the criminally

insane to the simply misguided, it wasn't about you. It didn't happen because you are bad or deserving of bad things, and nothing you could have done would have changed what happened.

3) Once you are clear on what happened and that it wasn't about you, it's time to forgive. This is the act of canceling the debt, granting the pardon and ceasing to feel resentment. This is easier when you understand that forgiving does not require you to say what happened is okay, or that you must allow the person who hurt you back in your life. You are not forgiving to help anyone but yourself. You don't even have to tell anyone else that you have forgiven that person.

4) Now it is time to release the hurt, anger and pain that are not serving you; and now that you have forgiven yourself and the other person, you can let it go. The person who hurt you has likely moved on. You deserve to be free of the negativity as well. If it helps, have a ceremony. Write down whatever it is you need to release on a piece of paper, take it to a quiet place, and burn the paper. Watch the paper that symbolizes your hurt turn to ash and then be carried away by the breeze.

5) The final step is to transform what happened to you into something beautiful. This can be whatever is meaningful to you. For Candy Lightner, whose thirteen year-old daughter Cari was killed by a drunk driver in 1980, it meant forming MADD®, a non-profit organization dedicated to changing public perception and policy about driving while impaired. Her efforts to change public perception about the dangers of impaired driving and advocate for laws that keep impaired drivers off the road have undoubtedly saved thousands of

people from having to experience the deep pain of losing a child at the hands of a drunk driver, like she did.[13] You don't have to create a national non-profit organization to make something beautiful happen. You can simply make sure you don't repeat the behavior. For example, if your father beat you, you can use the fear that you felt to stop you from ever striking a child. Refuse to make any child feel the same terror you felt. Making what hurt you beautiful helps with the release and forgiveness by providing a positive focus for your thoughts and energy.

You Are Currently Facing Significant Personal Issues

What is upsetting you can hurt your ability to effectively parent your child. Your child doesn't deserve to be hurt any more than you did when you were a child. Everyone can have a bad day, but if you find that you are being reactive, emotional, critical, demanding or abusive to your child, you need to stop. You can't just push through and hope that things will go back to normal once you feel better. Each time you behave badly as a parent, you not only hurt your child, you undermine your own credibility. This transfers your power to your child.

If you need help, ask for it. For particularly stressful situations, such as a divorce or loss of a loved one, you may need advice from a counselor or pastor and assistance from friends and family to help care for your child. Don't grin and bear it and go it alone, because

---

[13] MADD® official Web site, "About Us" page, "History of the Mission Statement," http://www.madd.org/about-us/mission/ (accessed February 15, 2012).

you don't have to.

Your Child's Behavior Is Extreme

Keeping your power requires you to make conscious parenting decisions – responding to your child, not reacting. This is easier when there is no conflict. However, when your child is angry, defiant, obstinate, hurtful or otherwise acting out, you are more likely to react to her behavior. If her behavior is extremely challenging, you will constantly battle your own emotions and reactive impulses in addition to having to address her behavior. This can be exhausting both physically and emotionally.

Understanding your child's behavior, what motivates it and how best to deal with it as described in Chapter 6 will be critical to your ability to parent her and feel successful. Remembering that her behavior is not personal will enhance your ability to remain calm. Your child has extra needs and will require more from you than the typically-developing child. In order to take care of her, you will need to make sure your needs are also being met. Be extra vigilant about self-care, asking for help and taking breaks.

A friend of mine with an autistic son is a divorced parent of two children. She also has a full-time job. In the past, she struggled to make sure her son's tremendous needs were met without neglecting her other child, her work and herself. She has since reached out to family and friends and worked out a schedule that includes frequent visitors, play dates for her son, one-on-one time with her daughter and a monthly 24-hour break for herself. She finds that she is able to handle the stress and demands better when she knows everyone's needs are met and she will have time alone to recharge every month.

Pause – Pause Longer if You Are Upset

Remember that the distance between a stimulus or provocation and a response is time and thought. If you don't take the time to stop and think, you are more likely to be reactive rather than responsive. The more upset or angry you are, the longer the pause needs to be.

When dealing with provocation from my teens, I found it useful to silently count to ten. While silently counting, I took a few deep breaths, looked at my child calmly and gathered my resolve. After counting, I took the time to think about what she said and formulate a response. This could take another five to ten seconds. That's a really long time for an angry teen to be facing a calm, unruffled parent. Often, before I even started talking, she retracted the request or apologized for acting inappropriately. Counting to ten is a parenting tool that is truly a win-win because it helps everyone stay calm, encourages the child to practice self-discipline and keeps the parent from being reactive.

9

Ignore It and It Will Go Away

When most of us become parents, our childrearing training typically consists of reading a book or two and discussing problems as they arise with a pediatrician or family member. Our default parenting style is typically exactly the same as or the polar opposite of how our parents raised us. We're all in this together, and we're all doing the best we can with parenting credentials accumulated through on-the-job training.

Why is this so when parenting is a job that more than four out of five adults will have? I doubt many would argue that childrearing training isn't necessary because the job is easy or unimportant. Possibly there is a widespread assumption that our childhood experience in a family environment is sufficient to prepare us to be good parents. This is clearly a better theory when the family of origin is healthy and functional, but that isn't always the case; and it isn't enough to assume that all parents will benefit from a good foundation based on early, positive role modeling. Even those with strong childhood family experiences are likely to lack all the tools they need to be successful as parents. It is even more likely, however, that there is no training or emphasis on parenting education because it hasn't been established as a priority – with resources and leadership to make it available to everyone.

I'm Doing the Best I Can

What we have is a multitude of parents with the belief that it will all work out and our children will be okay if we just do the best we can. Accepting this idea is one of the most common mistakes that parents make, and I believe we are set up to accept it as true. If no training is needed, we must all be ready and able to do the job, right?

How does the "it will all work out in the end if I just do my best" strategy fail us as parents? Nature follows the path of least resistance. Think of a riverbed: the path of least resistance will lead from point A to point B, but won't necessarily be the most efficient or well-thought-out path. Even worse, point B may not be a good place. Parenting requires more.

To understand how we are lulled by the concept of nature taking its course, think back to when your child was an infant. From the very first day, we dislike hearing our children cry. Whether it's a piercing wail of pain or a long-winded, whiny sob at night, the sound of a child's cry moves parents to action. It's natural and perfectly fine to react to it, but what happens if your reaction becomes an unthinking response that doesn't change and mature over time, with your child? This is where you may end up following the path of least resistance instead of creating the path that is best for your child.

A baby aged eighteen to thirty-six months has learned that making a lot of noise and being persistent sometimes gets him what he wants. If he knows Mom or Dad is motivated primarily to stop the crying, then crocodile tears are all the currency he needs.

I was at the doctor's office with my twenty-one-month-old son, who was suffering with a cold that had taken a turn for the worse.He is generally good-natured, and will tolerate a lot of poking and prodding until you stick something in his ear. Once he sees the scope moving toward his head, he starts fighting for his life. Now that he is getting stronger, the doctor asked my husband and me to help tame the tiger so that he could have both hands free to get a good look. My husband took the top half of my son and I clamped down on his chubby little thighs to keep him from thrashing and kicking his way off the table. He sobbed, screamed "no," and attempted to escape restraint for the entire fifteen seconds it took the doctor to peek at his eardrums. He cried the biggest tears I have ever seen, and if I hadn't been in the room to witness events myself I would have thought the poor baby had been tortured. Although he didn't get what he wanted, he was immensely successful in creating a drama featuring him as the pitiful victim that needed rescuing. He clearly did not want the doctor to check his ears, but we just as clearly could not give him what he wanted without risking his health. A few hugs and kisses were he needed for his tears to dry up as quickly as they had appeared.

I use our story as an example because it describes a situation that is pretty easily recognizable as one where a parent, no matter how uncomfortable she is with the crying and carrying on, has to momentarily ignore a child's distress in order to give him the proper medical care he needs. I wasn't oblivious or completely unmoved by my son's cries; I just had to act in his best interest and refuse to give in to what he wanted.

For most parents, overlooking a child's distress is difficult, and some are not able to. I was at a cocktail party with a group of friends where a mom, almost proudly, recounted a story in which she was unable to stay in the room with her wailing child who was having blood drawn because she couldn't stand to hear her baby cry. Others were very sympathetic and joined in with their own "I know this has to be done for my child's well-being, but I can't stand to be in the room and hear him cry" versions of the tale. All of the me-toos came from moms, while the rest of us moms and all of the dads checked out the paint on the ceiling. What can be said in polite conversation? I know it isn't the most pleasant part of our job as parents to see our children in distress, but isn't it harder to leave your sobbing child than to bear your own pain and stay there to provide as much comfort as you can? Isn't it weak and selfish to leave the room? If you can't bear to see your child cry when he's reacting to what is obviously necessary and for his own good, you have no chance when the issue is bedtime or a piece of candy before dinner.

Even with the rest of us who are able to restrain our crying children in a doctor's office, there are still some for whom the issue gets murkier when the drama is just as loud and insistent but the child's object of desire is not related to health or safety. Giving your child what he wants is easier in the moment because it stops the bad behavior, and it is often easy to justify it with "just this once," or "he's just really tired," or "one cookie before lunch won't really hurt him." After all, you want your child to be happy – and if it takes giving in to him on just this teeny little issue or just this one time, what's the harm?

It's No Fun to Have to Say No

It's not wrong to want your child to be happy. However,

momentary happiness is not the goal. Babies aged eighteen to thirty-six months who have learned that a little commotion and crocodile tears can get them what they want have a very hard time self-regulating later on. They rely more heavily on others or circumstances to set limits and have a very difficult time if they are not instantly gratified. Obviously not what you want for your child, but it's a future that can't be seen that is traded for the comfort of the moment. Children at this age that are not provided with appropriate and consistent boundaries suffer the most, because they haven't learned the most basic skill of self-control. That is a skill that is very difficult to learn later on. The path of least resistance is the road to giving your child what he wants, rather than teaching him self-control and responsibility.

Nature left unrestrained will always take its course. However, you may not like where nature ends up. Many parents are lulled into inaction by thinking that the momentary pain will work itself out. It will, but it will be along the path of least resistance, which is unlikely to end with the best outcome. If you have been lulled into believing that it will all work out eventually, this is your wake up call. Left to "it will all work out in the end if I just do my best," your child will wander the path of least resistance with lots of twists and turns and a final destination determined by the lowest elevation. If you engage, you can help your child to a better place.

10

I Want Her to Like Me

As parents willing to make personal sacrifices and spend considerable emotional and physical energy to make sure our children are protected and lovingly cared for, it seems inconceivable that anyone, much less the children who are beneficiaries of all the effort, would object. Unfortunately, our children don't see the world the way we do. This is especially true of entitled children. Your child is looking at the tactical or day-to-day events – the "how" – and you are focused on the strategic or big picture plan – the "why." Your child's focus, and whether or not she is happy or agrees with your decisions, is based on her short-term needs and wants. She won't be able to appreciate the longer- term importance of your decisions, and you can't give in to her because she is unhappy in the here and now.

You will definitely have to make her unhappy at times in the short-term to accomplish the long-term goal of raising a healthy, well-adjusted child. When you understand deeply that your job will include making decisions she doesn't agree with, you will recognize that you are doing your job well if she is unhappy with you at times. You will also be better able to resist the temptation to give in to her against your better judgment, or feel the need to justify and explain your position until she understands and agrees with you. What do you remember about your parents' decisions, and how often you agreed or were happy with them? If you were not spoiled as a child, you knew your parents would set boundaries you didn't like and tell you no at times. In fact, it is possible that being in agreement with your parents, while a nice bonus if it happened, was not your expectation. However, you respected their authority, appreciated their care and loving concern and accepted their direction, for the most part. As you grew and matured, you were better able to see the bigger picture and appreciate their guidance, even if you still didn't agree with all their decisions. That's what happens in the best-case scenario, and can set the stage for a parent to discipline without fear and guilt getting in the way. Even so, some who experienced great role models while growing up turn into spoiler parents by going overboard in an effort to make sure their children have it better than they did.

If your parents were more punitive, reactive, harsh or detached, however, you may have felt so unheard and unhappy that you decided to shield your child from what you once experienced. Instead of looking to establish a firm but loving environment, you may have decided that you want your child to be happy and to give her what she wants without considering the impact on her future well-being. At the opposite extreme, if you were spoiled as a child you had and may still have a low tolerance for frustration, and may be unwilling to expose your own child to short-term disappointment.

It may be helpful to look at an example. How many times has your child argued with you or resisted bedtime? If your child is like mine, it is more times than you can count. She is interested and engaged in what she is doing in the moment and really could not care less about her body's need for rest and the consequences the next day if she doesn't get enough sleep. If your goal is to get her to be happy about going to bed, or to rationalize with her until she agrees with your decision about what time she needs to go to bed, you are both going to be awake for quite a while. If you bribe her in an effort to get her to be happy with going to bed, she will learn that she has power over you and that she can expect to profit from being uncooperative.

Knowing she won't always agree takes the issue off the table. Your child has to understand that you don't need her approval; you simply need her cooperation. Without the power to influence your decision with her cries, arguments and stall-tactics, she will quickly learn to follow the routine. You can still be flexible on occasion, as long as she knows that you are making an exception to reward her for her cooperation and good attitude.

Strategies for When She Doesn't Agree

You are now armed with knowledge that will help you resist the temptation to give in when your child doesn't agree with you:

1) You are ready because you know that she won't always agree with you

2) When she disagrees, it doesn't mean that you made a poor decision or that you need to negotiate with her

3) You know that you are more capable of making decisions that support her long-term welfare than she is

4) You understand that your job is to encourage her cooperation, not secure her agreement

Let's go over some of the things you will experience when she disagrees with you and get ready with some "brategies" (strategies for dealing with entitled behavior).

"You Don't Trust Me"

"You don't trust me" is my favorite. Oh, I trust you, darling. I trust you to behave like the teenager you are. Therein lies the problem. What she means is that you don't trust her to behave in a completely responsible and mature manner, and she's right. You don't and you shouldn't.

I remember this conversation with my second child when he was sixteen: he wanted permission to drive three of his friends to a high school basketball game being played several towns away. "Mom, it will be okay, I'm a good driver. Why don't you trust me?" he asked. He was convinced that his two months of solo driving experience qualified him to chauffeur three of his friends. I listened to his "you don't trust me" tirade for ten minutes, using my "oh" technique. When he wound down, the look in his eyes was one of challenge: tell me I'm wrong, Mom, and I won't believe you. So I looked him in those eyes and told him that I trusted him completely to act like a sixteen year-old driver with very limited experience behind the wheel, driving three rambunctious boys to a late-night game in a location that was unfamiliar to him. Oh.

It is extremely important not to argue with your child when she disagrees with you. By engaging with her, you give her the message that her opinion holds as much weight as yours does. An argument is simply an effort to convince another of your point of view. If you give your child the opportunity to argue with you, you also give her the message that she has a chance to sway your decision. If you disengage with her, you let her know that you are in charge and do not need her input or agreement. You can disengage by simply letting her know that you won't argue with her. A firm but loving statement is often all that is needed, such as, "I'm not going to argue with you about this. We can discuss it again when you are feeling calmer," or "I love you too much to argue. I know that you don't agree with me, but that is my decision."

If your daughter has asked to attend a sleepover and you want to consider letting her go, don't make it an issue of trust with her. Employ the doctrine "trust but verify" that Ronald Reagan used to great effect with the Soviet Union (one of the most notable times occurring during the INF Treaty signing in 1987).[14] We all remember what we were like as kids, but somehow our children think they are completely original. I remember the sleepover bait and switch. My friend and I would tell our respective parents that we were sleeping over at each other's houses, leaving us completely free to roam the town for the night and end up sleeping over at our wild friend's house. My parents never called my friend's mom to check. Not once. I was a pretty good kid, so my kind of trouble was not particularly bad; but the fact that my parents didn't bother to check on me was both liberating and lonely. A part of me felt like they really didn't care. Don't apologize for calling the other parents. You can check without checking. Be artful and ask if you can bring some breakfast treats over, or what the kids' plans are for the morning so that you know what time to expect your child home.

---

[14] Ronald Wilson Reagan, "Remarks at the Signing of the INF Treaty with Soviet Premier Gorbachev" (speech, White House, Washington, D.C., December 8, 1987), retrieved from the official Web site of the Miller Center at the University of Virginia, http://millercenter.org/president/speeches/detail/5866 (accessed February 15, 2012).

You'll either get a straightforward answer to your question, or you'll quickly find out that there's a caper going on.

Trust your child to act her age and then parent her accordingly. She's going to try to make you feel bad in an effort to get you to change your decision or give her what she wants. Engaging in an argument or attempting to persuade her with logic only serves to weaken your position as the one in charge.

"You Don't Love Me"

This is likely the most difficult thing to hear from your child – maybe even more hurtful than "I hate you." The chances that you will never hear either statement from your child are very remote. It can be shocking the first time you hear them, because you feel such attachment to and love for your child. It's inconceivable that she doesn't recognize that or feel the same way.

It's extremely important to use the skills from Chapter 8 and not overreact. It helps to understand that what your child means when she says, "You don't love me," or "I hate you," is really "I am very unhappy with you right now." It's easier to stay calm and respond to your child when you put her statement in context. If you lose control and react to "I hate you" by calling her ungrateful, hurling exaggerated insults back at her or otherwise engaging in an argument with her, you may create barriers in your relationship that will be difficult to overcome later.

My favorite tactic to use with over-dramatic statements from my children was always to diffuse them with a low-key reply. My response to "I hate you" or "You don't love me" was often, "Okay, but I still love you." Using humor is very effective as well, because it gets your point across and lightens the mood. You know your child. You know how to appeal to her when she's angry or not feeling her best. Put some thought and your personality into a few good responses that you can have ready when she gets dramatic. Instead of losing your cool, you can model appropriate behavior, take the focus off her dramatic statement and get back onto the real issue at hand. Chapter 14 will cover this in more detail, with specific tips and solutions.

She Questions Your Authority

Whether you are dealing with a stubborn two year-old, a defiant teen or an obstinate adult child, if you have been a spoiler parent, you have given her too much power in your relationship. She questions your authority and pushes you to give her even more power because that gets her what she wants. She is going to continue to question your authority and push you to get her way until that tactic no longer works for her. You are not going to be able to convince her that you will no longer be a spoiler parent; you are going to have to demonstrate it to her.

This means that you are going to have to be a leader. You will need to model for her that you are responsible and able to control your emotions, that you are responsive vs. reactive, and that you are acting in the best interest of every family member. You can't expect her to behave in a respectful and responsible manner if you are not capable of or willing to do the same. You will need to be able to inspire her to do her best. This can only be done in a supportive and encouraging environment where every family member feels like a part of the team.

George S. Patton put it very succinctly when he said, "We herd sheep, we drive cattle, we lead people."[15] If you are being a spoiler parent, you are not leading your child. If you do not lead her, you will have to push, drive or herd her, which can have very mixed results and may be the reason you decided to be a spoiler parent in the first place. You have another option, and that is to lead with strength. Your child will respect your authority if you behave as a leader: expect your child to behave well, put the boundaries and limits in place to increase her chances of success, and make sure you behave as an excellent role model.

Expect Her to Not Agree

If your child doesn't agree with you, it simply means you are not serving her immediate desires and she may be mad at you about that for a while. Now that you expect her to disagree with you at times and know that you don't have to change your mind or explain your position to her, much less get her to agree with you, you can continue to lead with purpose and refuse to engage her with arguments, bribes, spoiling or compromise. She needs your leadership, and she will challenge your authority with less frequency as you show her that you are a capable, responsible and loving parent.

---

[15] Kelly Nickell, ed., *Pocket Patriot: Quotes from American Heroes* (Cincinnati: F +W Publications, Inc., 2005), 157.

11

Really, It's Not That Bad

One of the biggest issues spoiler parents face is minimization. Minimization is the tendency to reduce the severity of a problem by denying its significance. For spoiler parents, it is the attempt to salvage denial when it is no longer possible to ignore the unpleasant facts. Minimizing helps ease the emotional burden of the situation because it significantly underrates the gravity of the problem. It's what happens when you can't deny that your child's entitled behavior is unacceptable, and you feel guilty for your own role in spoiling him. You feel better, or at least less awful, if you are able to avoid confrontation with the true extent of the problem.

Our children are great at minimizing as well. My son opened an umbrella in the garage while standing right next to his brother, who got poked in the face. Instead of apologizing and giving his brother a hug, he said, "I just opened the umbrella!" He couldn't deny that the umbrella opened, or that in the process of opening, it poked his brother, so he engaged in minimization (pairing justification with denial) to ease his guilt about hurting his brother due to carelessness.

What Does Minimization Sound Like?

Minimization may be what has allowed you to continue to spoil your child long after you have recognized that he is entitled. Have you ever found yourself saying any of the following?

1) His bad behavior is not that big of a deal
2) Don't all kids behave this way?
3) He usually behaves much better than this
4) He's just tired/bored/having a bad day
5) He's just high-spirited/stubborn/precocious

If you have thought or said any of the above, you have been minimizing his behavior to avoid dealing with it and to make yourself feel better as a parent.

Minimization, like placating your unruly child, has only temporary benefits. You will have peace in the moment, but as you refuse to acknowledge or address your child's entitled behavior, it will get worse and eventually be impossible to deny.

I have seen the motive for minimization change with the age of the entitled child.

Minimization When Your Child is 0-10

Parents of younger children are often just emotionally unable to accept that their child is capable of willful bad behavior. Who wants to believe that their child is born with more challenging characteristics or personality traits, and acts out more frequently as a result? And if you cling to the belief that your child is innately wonderful and perfect, then bad behavior must be a result of bad parenting – also not an idea that a newer parent wants to confront.

Minimizing the entitled behavior makes it "normal" and allows you to ignore the problem. However, the entitled behavior still needs to be dealt with on a daily basis, and because you haven't recognized it for what it is, you won't respond appropriately. This is an extreme example, but imagine a scenario in which public health officials respond to a highly contagious plague outbreak on a case-by-case basis, treating only the sick patients who show up at the hospital or clinic. Ignoring the bigger picture would only ensure a pandemic, with more and more people exposed and falling ill. A better response would involve alerting the public to the danger, quarantining those who are falling ill, restricting travel and using preventive medicines if available.

If you have normalized your entitled child's behavior, then you are dealing with his outbursts and bad behavior on a case-by-case basis. You may achieve peace in the moment, but you are likely resorting to placation, bribery, threats, harsh discipline or other techniques that will be ineffective in the long-term. You will both become frustrated, which will make it more likely that you will fall into the other traps (giving away your power, reacting, figuring the problem will eventually fix itself and expecting your child will agree) that are outlined in Chapters 7 through 10. Instead, start first with acknowledging the problem and resisting the temptation to minimize it.

Here's an example of minimizing with a young child that I witnessed while visiting with a friend several years ago. It illustrates how deeply we are influenced by the incredible cuteness of our young children.

My friend Anna noticed that her seven year-old daughter Kate refused to share with her friend. As Kate walked away, flashing her biggest smile, she announced that she couldn't share because that was the candy she got from Santa. Anna got up from the table, went to the cupboard and found a treat to give Kate's friend to smooth things over. Before we resumed our discussion, Anna, obviously feeling a little guilty for succumbing to Kate's manipulation, told me that Kate doesn't usually act that way. Because she minimized her daughter's behavior, she allowed herself to feel better about failing to address it. I had been around Anna and her daughter numerous times, and I knew that this was not the first (and would not likely be the last) time Kate exhibited entitled behavior.

Minimization When Your Child Is 10-20

If you have a pre-teen or older child, you are now less likely to believe that he is incapable of bad behavior. Part of the reason for this is your experience. You have had more parenting time with your child, and you have been exposed to other children both directly and by sharing experiences with other parents. You know that your child will act up.

Entitled behavior is less subtle at this age, making it very difficult to minimize with, "He doesn't normally act this way," or "He's just having a bad day." If you accept that your child's entitled behavior is a problem, then you have to confront your role in encouraging the behavior. This is very emotionally challenging to do, so many parents continue to minimize. Because it is now more difficult to minimize the child's increasingly blatant behavior, they minimize in other ways. This includes downplaying their own role in creating the entitled child, the availability of solutions or their own strength to address the problem. Here, minimization allows us to avoid taking responsibility for creating the problem or for solving it. If you have convinced yourself that there is no problem, that it's unsolvable or that you had little control over how your child became entitled, there's nothing for you to be responsible for. That feels better in the moment, but leaves your child without leadership and with the burden of entitled behaviors that are causing and will continue to cause him pain.

The most common form of minimization I hear from parents is, "I had no other choice." What this really means is that they don't know of another solution, they don't want to try an alternative or they feel too weak to discipline effectively.

Minimization When Your Child Is 20+

It may be difficult for some parents with an adult entitled child to recognize minimization because the pattern is so ingrained for both the spoiler parent and the spoiled child. Let's take the example of your son asking you for the money to fix the brakes on his car. You reason that if you don't give him the money to fix the brakes, he won't be able to go to work and make money; and then you'll really have a problem on your hands because he will move back home. Even worse, if you don't give him the money and he drives around on bad brakes, he may have an accident and hurt himself or someone else. For practical and safety-related reasons, you give him the $300. Makes perfect sense and you really did not have a choice as a responsible parent, right?

You do have a choice. As uncomfortable as it may be, you can make a decision to not rescue your adult son, leaving him to make his own decisions and be responsible for the outcomes, whether they are good or bad.

How Do You Know If You Are Minimizing?

Regardless of your child's age, you can recognize minimization if you find yourself in the following situations:

1) You are saying or thinking any of the following words: just, barely, sort of, no big deal, not more than, only a little, kind of, merely

2) You are attempting to shift or deny responsibility

3) You are at increased risk of minimization if you are experience intense negative emotions, such as guilt or fear

The first key to recognizing when you minimize behavior is word choice. "I just wanted him to be happy" is a minimization I have heard many times from spoiler parents. The key word is "just," which is a big tip-off that minimization is occurring. Wanting your child to be happy is clearly not the problem. Making decisions for your child aimed more toward making him happy than disciplining him appropriately certainly is.

The second key is transferring responsibility. This is simply an attempt to shield yourself and your child from the consequences of his actions. For example, if your eight year-old child takes a toy from the store without paying for it, you minimize the situation with, "He's too young to know any better." This absolves him of any responsibility for his actions, and absolves you if you neglected to teach him not to steal. A much better response would be to hold your child accountable for his actions by insisting that he return the item and apologize to the store manager.

Another good example of minimizing by shifting responsibility is what happens when a child gets aggressive with another child during a play date. "Those other children are simply too rough and bring out the worst in my child," is an attempt to shift responsibility from your child to other children. "My child hasn't been feeling well," is simply an attempt to deny that your child was responsible without placing blame on anyone else.

The third key to recognizing minimization is to be extra aware if you are feeling intense negative emotions, as minimization is a defense mechanism we use to protect ourselves from pain.[16] Consider an entitled child for whom socialization with other children is difficult due to his low frustration tolerance. He is demanding and bossy with other children, making it difficult for him to maintain friendships. His lack of friends and the fact that other children ostracize him at school is very painful for you both. If you find yourself saying, "Other children just don't understand you," or "I never got along with other children when I was your age," you are minimizing.

As noted at the beginning of this chapter, minimization is something we all do to lessen emotional pain. It only becomes unhealthy when it is overused and we fail to connect with our true experiences, thoughts and feelings. If you feel stuck as a spoiler parent and you see yourself in any of the situations described above, you are overusing this defense mechanism. For many, just recognizing the problem is all that is necessary to solve it. If you recognize minimization as a crutch that you no longer choose to lean on, you will refuse to let it influence the way you parent your child.

One of my clients has three adult entitled children and is a very

---

[16] Richard Niolon, PhD, "Defenses," official PsychPage Web site, April 18, 2001, http://www.psychpage.com/learning/library/counseling/defenses.html (accessed February 15, 2012).

accomplished high-level manager working for a large corporation. His wife is a teacher, also very respected in her profession. All three children live in their home, the youngest being twenty-four. In addition, their middle child is an unwed mother who is living there with her five year-old son. Having all three adult children in their home was not causing the couple financial stress, as they could afford to support their children and grandchild. However, they were starting to worry that their kids would never move out and become financially independent. They asked for my advice on how to encourage their children to move out, initially proposing that I meet with their children individually to educate them on financial responsibility. While I agreed to meet with the children, I suggested that it would be difficult for me or anyone else to convince these children to move out when their parents had made it so easy for them to stay. The parents weren't charging rent, regularly watched the grandchild (making it easy for their daughter to date and go away for long weekends) and kept the refrigerator well-stocked. They had an impressive list of minimizations, including, "All we did was love them" and "It's really not a big deal that they are still living at home." Once they understood that they were using minimization to avoid facing the reality of the situation, they immediately threw away the crutch. I reminded them of the talents and skills they used to great effect in the business world, and that those same talents could be lovingly applied in their home as well. Once they decided that their children would no longer get a free ride, all three moved out within six months. My clients continue to have loving relationships with all three, who are doing better now than they were while living off Mom and Dad.

If you are using minimization as a crutch because you feel you do not have the skills and resources to face the truth of having spoiled your child, I would encourage you to seek appropriate counseling. Parenting is a difficult job, one for which we sometimes need help and support.

If you have recognized minimization as one of the traps you have fallen into as a spoiler parent, you have taken the first and most important step to correct the problem. Now that you no longer minimize the degree of the entitlement problem, you will be motivated to find solutions. As a mature adult, you are well equipped with many skills and talents that can be used to help your child once you face the entitlement problem with clarity. Without the minimization crutch, you will be fully ambulatory and energetic in helping your child as a disciplined parent.

12

Her Happiness Is Everything to Me

We don't like to see her cry. It hurts us to see her disappointed, frustrated, upset, embarrassed or injured. Because of our instinct to love and protect, we are vulnerable to making the most common mistake made by spoiler parents, which is to use our love for our children to justify actions or inactions that result in overprotection, spoiling or rescuing. We are effectively blinded by love, and as a result fail to make the strong parenting decision in favor of one that coddles or insulates. When we love too much or in the wrong way, we hurt instead of help our children.

Do You Love Her So Much You Are Hurting Her?

If any of the following sound familiar, you may have fallen into the hurting trap:

1) I feel responsible for helping her because I made decisions or mistakes that hurt her in the past – I need to make it up to her now

2) I only do things for her because I want her to be happy

3) I have to help because she isn't able to do it for herself

4) It's my fault she doesn't know how to take care of herself

5) She still needs me to take care of her

6) I can afford it, so why shouldn't I take care of her financially?

7) It causes me too much worry and stress to let her handle her own affairs – it's easier on me if I intervene and make sure she is taken care of

8) I have to make sure nothing bad happens to her

Parents who love so much it hurts are typically doing it for one of two reasons. The first is out of a desire to make sure she doesn't get hurt. You have felt pain and don't want her to have to suffer like you did. The second reason is that you feel guilty or fearful and are coddling her so you can feel better.

If you are just trying to make sure she doesn't get hurt and you are a typical overprotective parent, as described by Sarah Briggs in "Confessions of a Helicopter Parent," you may relate to the mantra, "Never leave anything to chance."[17] Helicopter parents want to make sure their child's path is cleared of obstacles, and to ensure her safety so that she doesn't experience painful situations or emotions. They want the best for their child and are very focused on ensuring that she is happy and never wants for anything.

On the other hand, if you are parenting out of fear or guilt, you

---

[17] Sarah Briggs, "Confessions of a Helicopter Parent," official Experience.com Web site, http://www.experience.com/alumnus/channel? channel_id=parents_survival_guide&page_id=helicopter_parents (accessed February 15, 2012).

may have adopted a helicopter parenting style to protect yourself, especially if your guilt or fear relates to your own personal baggage as described in Chapter 3. However, there are other fears that motivate a parent to adopt helicopter mode. These include the following:

1) The world is too harsh, or your child is too weak or unprepared to be successful without your interference

2) She won't love you anymore if you refuse her

3) You will be responsible or she will blame you for her lack of success if you don't give her what she wants

Were you afraid to let her be herself and make some mistakes along the way? It's hard to watch your child fail or be disappointed. Did that make you so uncomfortable that you swooped in to fix everything for your child, not because it was in her best interest, but because you couldn't stand how you were feeling? Let's say your daughter can be a bit bossy. It happens. There's the part of you that doesn't like the overbearing part of her, but then there's the part that sees her as the adorable girl that can do no wrong. When she was rude and bossy to her playmates, did you try to smooth it over and then plan future play dates with "nicer" kids? Were those nicer kids in reality just pushovers who didn't stand up to her and teach her valuable lessons about getting along and self-sacrifice? If so, you lost sight of your job. Without realizing it, you taught her that her bossy behavior will be tolerated rather than teaching her the skills she needs to get along with others.

Are You Just Trying to Save Her From Herself?

As the spoiler parent of an adult child, you are still trying to protect her from her own mistakes and bailing her out from the consequences of her actions. As long as you do that, she will be free to be lazy and irresponsible and to make poor choices. Not what you want, but that's what will happen.

I was working with a retired couple facing some cash flow issues. They had decent retirement income, but their expenses had gotten higher and they were dipping into savings at an unsustainable rate. When we reviewed their expenses, they revealed that they were paying rent and taking care of a car payment, insurance and a cell phone bill for their twenty-five year-old son who was living on his own, not in school and working full-time. What a sweet deal. They had co-signed on the loan for the car, so they felt they needed to keep up with the car payments and insurance to preserve their own credit. But why the rent and the $250 per month cell phone bill? Because he couldn't have any fun if he had to use all his money to pay bills. No kidding, that was their explanation.

In trying to be loving and supportive for their son, his parents were actually crippling him. He had no problem taking money from them, but became resentful when he felt he wasn't free to spend the money he earned without his parents looking over his shoulder. Because he had always been subsidized, he had no incentive to solve his own problems or make tough choices. He convinced them that having a roommate was too difficult, a second job too taxing, a better job impossible and living without the extras inconceivable. He even had his parents convinced that a $250 cell phone service was vital to his well-being and active social life. So they had agreed to solve his cash flow problem, and yet they were fighting about money with him constantly. He wanted more things and they wanted to give him less money; he was resentful that they asked too many questions and they felt they had the right to pry since they were paying many of his bills.

When I dug further into their rationale for paying over $1,500 per month to support their son when they could not afford to do so, it was clear this was a case of loving so much it hurt – all of them. This was not about their desire to make sure he had fun. They felt guilty that his financial irresponsibility was their fault because they had not taught him about money. Additionally, they were afraid of his reaction and what would happen to their relationship with him if they stopped sending the checks. They traded their parent power for his affection.

I helped them understand that even if they could have done a better job preparing him to be financially responsible, giving him money now is making matters worse, not better. And what if he does get mad at them when they stop paying his bills? He can't stay mad forever. Once he figures out how to solve his own problems and pay his own way, he'll feel better about himself and maybe even appreciate what it took for his parents to stop enabling him to be a sponge. He may realize that they actually did him a favor by cutting off the gravy train and expecting him to take care of himself.

If you are paying for essentials, or if it seems too harsh or scary to say no, you can phase in the new rules. Many spoiler parents have told me that they haven't asked their child to pay rent or move out because they worry their child will be homeless. The solution is a phase-in period that includes advance notice of a month or two, followed by a few months during which nominal rent is charged, and then rent at market price. I have yet to hear of client's child who chooses to live at home instead of move out and live on her own when the cost is about the same.

If you now have the resolve to say no but fear that your child will act out or that you will crumble when she throws a tantrum, there are some terrific parenting resources available. You can get recommendations on parenting strategies from your pediatrician, mental health professional or minister. There are also parenting workshops available through community organizations, churches and mental health providers. One of my favorite parenting strategies is the "Parenting With Love and Logic" program, founded by Jim Fay and Foster W. Cline. This program offers parents an "approach to raising kids that provides loving support from parents while at the same time expecting kids to be respectful and responsible."[18] Having a framework and support in place before you decide to make a significant change in the way you parent your child will increase your chances of success. You simply have to realize that it is more loving to stop your overindulgent or overprotective behavior than to keep her dependent on you. If she's depending on you to make all her decisions and protect her from the consequences of her actions, she will not mature emotionally. What she needs more than your money or your coddling is to know that you believe in her and trust her ability to solve her own problems and make good choices. She needs to be able to make mistakes, pick herself back up and try something else without your interference. It's the truly loving thing to do for your child.

---

[18] Love and Logic® official Web site "Home" page, "What is Love and Logic® for Parents?" http://www.loveandlogic.com/what-is-for-parents.html (accessed February 15, 2012).

End of Part Two

Part Three

What Do I Do Now?

13

Kid Basics

Now that you have learned how you got here and what went wrong (you gave away your power, you were in reactive mode, you thought the problem would go away on its own, you were overly concerned about him liking you, you minimized the situation and loved him too much), here are six solutions that will increase your confidence and ability to move from spoiler to disciplined parent.

Identify Family Values and Build Character

We shape our child's character over time, through storytelling, teaching, modeling and providing discipline. Each child is unique, with his own temperament, talents and personality, and each needs to be artfully sculpted to bring out his best qualities. The goal of childrearing is to develop a happy, mature, responsible, kind adult. Building good character is essential to this goal, and can only be done with strong values in place.

I would like to encourage you to put some time into thinking about what values are important to you. When I need inspiration, I look to classic sources and to those who have achieved great success. A good place to begin is by looking at the seven deadly sins, because they are fatal to the building of character: lust, gluttony, greed, slothfulness, wrath, envy and pride. This list is drawn from Christian teachings, but philosophies that address character can be pulled from many sources, including other religions and Greek mythology.

For each of the seven deadly sins, there is a corresponding virtue. These virtues are chastity, temperance, charity, diligence, patience, kindness and humility. Character is what defines us. Having good character is what makes us willing to practice diligence instead of slothfulness, or to act with humility versus pride. The question each parent must ask herself is, "What do I value, and what characteristics do I want my child to possess?" It is helpful to make a list. Don't be concerned with making it perfect, as you can always make changes. If it helps, just start with what you have and add to the list as you think of other values you would like your family to follow.

If you have been too permissive in an attempt to be accepting, tolerant and inclusive, you have left your child wondering what you stand for and what behavior is and is not acceptable. This makes character development difficult, if not impossible. In today's culture, where it is common practice to accept all behaviors as long as nobody gets hurt, it can seem old-fashioned or out-of-touch to clearly identify, model and teach values. You don't have to be judgmental about the choices other people make, but you do have to stand for the ideals you want to foster in your own home. If not, you create a laissez-faire environment in which your child will rightly conclude that anything goes.

Vince Lombardi, the legendary coach of the Green Bay Packers football team known for his soft-spoken and easy-going manner, developed a culture of discipline and integrity that produced champions and a champion team. In an article on CSBComSportsBiz.com, Cam Suarez-Bitar describes how Coach Lombardi "led by example and emphasized discipline, fearlessness, confidence, vision and direction, practicality, responsibility, honesty, commitment, power, and integrity."[19] Lombardi identified the values that he thought were crucial to building a winning team, clearly communicated them to his players, led by example and did not tolerate contradictory behavior from his team members.

Once you have identified the values that are important to you, you are ready to follow Coach Lombardi's example and use them in rearing your child. You don't have to be Coach Lombardi to be successful; you just need to be consistent and unwavering.

You Are a Powerful Teacher

Now that you now have identified the values that will serve as the foundation for character-building in your home, it is important to review the power you have as a parent. If you have become discouraged and doubt your ability to influence your child's behavior and effect change, he will sense your weakness, making it very difficult for you to implement and sustain change.

If you feel that you have not been effective as a parent or that your child doesn't listen to you or care what you say, you are probably basing this on the results of your past efforts. That does mean that what you have been doing hasn't worked, but it doesn't

---

[19] Cam Suarez-Bitar, "Vince Lombardi's Leadership and the Path to Wisdom," Communications on Sports Business official Web site, November 16, 2011, http://csbcomsportsbiz.com/2009/11/16/vince-lombardis-leadership-and-the-path-to-wisdom/ (accessed February 15, 2012).

mean you can't change your approach with some new skills that could change the outcome.

Shower with Positive Attention to Reinforce Learning and Cooperation

It's important to remember that all children crave approval and attention from their parents, and you increase his ability to learn and cooperate if you fulfill this need. Even if your child is in his twenties or beyond, he still wants to feel that you are proud of him and that he can count on you. Although you love him to pieces, he may have heard more negative messages from you about his behavior than positive ones.

You may be thinking that there's nothing to be positive about when it comes to your child's behavior, or that the bad behavior so outweighs the good, there's no way to tip the scale in a positive direction. You will be able to find the good as soon as you start looking. Your child's future depends on it. He may have taken extra time to help a friend with homework, helped a neighbor corral an escaped dog, made a sweet comment about someone – anything with a positive tone counts. The harder you look, the more you will find. Take a moment to make a list of all the wonderful qualities, special talents and beautiful things your child possesses and has done. Make sure the list isn't all ancient history, and that it doesn't focus on external qualities over which your child has no control. His beautiful smile is great for the list, because you love it and you want to see it more often. Focusing on his perfect teeth is less desirable for this list, because it's a physical characteristic over which he has no control. It won't feel as special to him if you notice his straight teeth versus his beautiful smile. You also need to be able to find current good qualities, or you won't be able to sound genuine when you start changing the game with positive attention.

Most parents find that showering a child with love and positive attention is natural and fun. Though it's a little more difficult with a child who is acting out, it is even more crucial. We all know an engine needs to be periodically maintained and well-lubricated if we don't want it to break down. Without lubrication, the pistons moving inside the engine cause too much friction and excessive wear, and this can cause the engine to break down completely. Think of positive attention as the lubrication your child needs to run smoothly. Negative words are like draining all the oil from the engine. It needs to be refilled quickly with positive ones. I don't know if there is a tried-and-true ratio, but I do know that it takes many positive words to counteract just one negative comment. Love your child, let him know that you can't imagine your life without him, tell him he's wonderful the way he is. That doesn't mean everything he does is wonderful or that you won't be frustrated with him at times. He'll know you're not happy when he's acted out, so make sure he knows that you are unhappy with his behavior and not with him as a person.

How to Teach Without Being Preachy

Teaching and preaching both involve imparting wisdom or knowledge from the more educated to those less learned. Both teachers and preachers typically have a sincere interest in the welfare of their students and a firm belief in the instruction material. Teaching typically veers into preaching when there is an unyielding fervor in the subject matter that is sometimes accompanied by a superior attitude toward the student. If you are communicating, "I don't care what you think because I know better," or "You will agree with me when you are older," your child will understand that you don't value his opinion or feelings and he will tune you out. You are more experienced and wise, but if you go preachy, he won't hear a word you say.

One of the best chances you'll have to teach without being preachy is when your child is having friend trouble. I call it a "friend talk," and it is a powerful way to teach children values that will stay with them. Because you are talking about someone else, your child is more likely to absorb the information without being defensive. Let's say your child's friend Eric is very opinionated. Your son doesn't like how Eric is so passionate about his ideas that he seems completely uninterested in what your son thinks. It makes him feel unappreciated. As you talk to your son about Eric and discuss strategies that Eric could use that would make him a better friend and listener, your child will be absorbing this. You won't be able to impact Eric, but through him you can help you son learn what it means to be a good listener. Maybe your son isn't the best listener either, and he'll start adopting some strategies you suggested for Eric. If humility is one of your family values, this would also be an excellent opportunity to stress its importance.

Through friendships with other children, your child will learn which qualities he appreciates in others and those he's not so crazy about. Your child will need this skill to use in the dating game, so it's crucial that he gets practice before his hormones kick in. It's also important that he understands that just because he doesn't appreciate a characteristic such as "too talkative," doesn't mean that person is wrong, or that someone else won't love that he talks so much.

Sometimes you will have to help your child understand that a friendship is no longer healthy. My advice to my children regarding friendship is:

1) Have fun and be yourself, and be friends with those who love who you are
2) Be a good friend and you will have good friends
3) Do not tolerate ongoing hurtful or negative behavior from a friend – it's sad to lose a friend, but it's much worse to deal with a bad relationship every single day.

In all the friend talks, I learned a great deal about my children. Even more importantly, they started to develop some awareness of their own characteristics and how others perceive them. Without self-awareness, the world can be a very frustrating place. If your child isn't able to recognize or accept how his own role has led to his difficulties, he isn't going to have much success in solving them.

Teach By Asking Questions Instead of Giving Answers

Now that you are no longer spoiling your child, you may hear, "It's not fair!" more than ever before. Simply stating that life isn't fair and he'd better get used to it may be somewhat realistic, but also a little harsh and beyond his grasp. When your child is feeling picked on or that the world is unjust, you have a wonderful opportunity to help him. Don't give him the answers. Instead, ask him questions. Some great questions are:

1) Why do you think that happened?
2) What would you do differently next time?
3) How can you make it better now?

As he learns to solve his own problems, you'll hear less "It's not fair!" At the same time, you'll be teaching him self-reliance and positive coping skills.

Use Humor Liberally

One of my favorite kid complaints is, "Everyone else gets to." It's the reason he should get the cell phone upgrade, be able to stay out until midnight on a school night, go to an unsupervised party and have you spring for the $200 pair of sneakers. Every family has different priorities and standards, but yours definitely won't be the same as everyone else's or you're going to have to beat all the Joneses. It's not something you should do even if you can afford it, because your child won't appreciate your sacrifices or understand limits as a result.

Humor is always an effective parenting tool, and I love to use it with "Everyone else gets to." So here's my favorite line. "You have the meanest Mom ever. I'm so sorry." "But Mom," he may protest. "No really, sweetie, I know all the other moms are nice and you got me. That's rough. And you still can't stay out until midnight tonight."

You can see his brain doing gymnastics. Worst case, if he's really angry, he'll agree with you and stomp off. "Everyone gets to" is just as absurd as you being "the worst mom ever." If he doesn't get the point right away, he will. Eventually he may even laugh. "Nobody likes me." This one is hard to hear. And the fact that you like him isn't going to count right now. He needs to feel included and accepted by his peers, and kids can be mean. But giving in and buying the $200 sneakers isn't going to help him either. He may be cool for the moment, but you can't solve a peer pressure problem with a pair of shoes.

During the teen years, your child is figuring out who he is and what his priorities are. All that can change quickly and often. He may outgrow his nerdy friend or tire of his group of friends that only think about girls. The changes will cause him to doubt himself, but you can help him to appreciate and even celebrate them. Use a humorous example like diapers. Sure, they were necessary, and at the time, perfectly comfortable; but you don't want to wear them forever because you won't need them once you learn to use the potty.

Have a Plan Before You Start

You are going to rock his world when you transition from spoiler to disciplined parent. As I mentioned before, he isn't going to like the changes and he will ramp up his behavior in an effort to dissuade you from following through. It's worked for him in the past, so he expects that it will work again, even if it takes longer this time. You will have to outlast him. Be committed to your values. Use them to guide you as you build his character. Make sure you keep your list of values handy, review it regularly and update it if you need to. Recognize that you are a powerful teacher and that you have immense influence in your child's life. Use encouragement, positive feedback and humor liberally. Use teaching moments to reinforce your family values, make sure your child knows you will always listen and ask questions instead of providing answers. Take the time to build a solid foundation to avoid a shaky start as a disciplined parent. Like Coach Lombardi, you can focus on your plan and lead a team of champions!

14

Be the Rock

The next solution, simply stated, is, "Be the rock." Be stable, firm, consistent and present. You child is the polar opposite of a rock. She is immature, underdeveloped, fickle and constantly testing limits. She needs you to be a rock to feel secure.

Your child's job is to test you. By pushing you, and by noting your response to her, she learns where the boundaries are and who will enforce them. As she reaches new developmental stages, she'll need to test again for new limits. Her job of testing will continue throughout her childhood. You can only influence whether her need to test will be calmed by consistent and loving discipline, or whether you encourage her to challenge you further by being inconsistent or unclear.

Have you ever known a family in which the mother is a very loving but firm disciplinarian, while the father is weak and permissive? A child in this home will push and challenge the father, creating chaos that can be restored by a firm word from the mother. This child understands that her mother has established clear boundaries, so there's no reason to continue testing them. On the other hand, her father has no rules and can be pushed.

Your child is really going to test you if you have decided to put on your big parents pants, take back your power and stand up to her demands now. It will be critical for you to stay composed. That doesn't mean that you have to deny your feelings – you shouldn't be stone cold, you just have to express your feelings in a way that is respectful and responsible.

What Does It Look Like to Be the Rock?

Think of yourself as a very large rock, partially submerged in the water. Your child is a dolphin, interested in playing and exploring the ocean. It's her job to explore, develop her skills and test her endurance. But she always comes back to you. She knows you will be there because you are the rock. It's easier to be the rock when you understand that it's her job to swim off and test her limits, because you expect her to explore and push the boundaries. It's not personal when she does; it's just her doing her job.

It's important to stay composed and calm, because children learn lessons from what we are proactively trying to teach them, from what we model for them and from what we fail to do. All three are equally important. If your child tests her limits and you overreact, tell her that you can't deal with her and her father will be home soon to punish her, or berate her, you model inappropriate behavior. On the other hand, if you are the rock and you expect her to test her limits, you won't be surprised by her behavior. This will make it much easier for you to remain calm.

Our children know when we mean business. My oldest has always been the mother hen to her brother, who is twenty-six months younger than she is. I often had to remind her that she needed to be the sister and I would take care of the mommy job.

When she was around six years old, we were shopping at the grocery store. We turned into an aisle where a mom was dealing with a three year-old pitching a fit over some cookies that she wanted her mom to buy. We were in the aisle for a couple of minutes and heard the entire fit. We saw the mother wear down and finally toss the cookies into the cart, screaming, "Are you happy now?" at her child. Clearly the mother was frustrated, but her unspoken lesson was: if you pitch a big enough fit, I'll give you what you want.

My daughter took the opportunity to turn this into an actual lesson for her four year-old brother. She put her hand on her hip and informed him that he should never try something like that because he would get a time-out instead of the cookies. The exchange between my children was priceless, and I was amused to think that it was possible my six year-old had a better idea of how to deal with naughty behavior than the frustrated mom. If you are the rock, your child will be comforted by your consistency and able to apply it to her world.

Tools to Help You Be the Rock

The more extreme the behavior your child throws at you, the more difficult it is to be the rock, even when you know it's her job to test you.

The Power of "Oh"

I believe that "oh" is one of the best words in the English language. It is a non-committal, non-judgmental way to say, "I heard you." It's an essential tool when dealing with angry children. They get to talk, you listen, and you don't need to take the trouble to comment when they aren't interested in your opinion or are too keyed up to be able to comprehend what you're saying.

Certainly you don't want to overuse "oh," or you will seem disengaged and uninterested. However, when your child is highly charged and needing to vent, it's the perfect word. For example, your teen just got home from school and is mad at you because you refused to run her forgotten lunch to school. She had to borrow scraps from friends and is now extremely hungry, and it's "all your fault." "Oh," you say. Hmmm, what does she say now? She vents a little more. She may even say you're the worst mom in the world. "Oh." Wow, no reaction from Mom, what's going on? She tries a few more digs. "Oh." Well that didn't work. "Hey Mom, didn't you hear what I just said?" she asks. She's calm enough now for you to talk with. You were giving her the courtesy of letting her tell you how she feels, and now it's your turn. You need her to know that remembering her lunch is her responsibility and you are not going to bring it to her if she forgets it. You can talk to her about ways she can take responsibility and help herself, such as by posting a school checklist on a whiteboard on the garage door. You want her to be successful and you don't want her to go hungry, but you aren't going to take responsibility for something she is capable of doing for herself.

Take a Deep Breath

How do you do this if you are really angry at her? It still can be done; it's just more difficult. The key is to let no words fly out of your mouth unedited. Count to ten, take a few deep breaths – whatever it takes to be sure that you are in control of your emotions when you speak. Start with telling her that you are angry. She needs to know that you can be angry and not lash out or be hurtful. You are modeling the behavior that you would like her to adopt. Do you want her to raise her voice and say hurtful things? Of course not! So you can't either.

Take the previous example, when she blamed you for the consequences of her own actions and said you are the worst mom in the world. Tell her that it makes you sad that she would try to blame you for something that she should be taking responsibility for. You get that it's no fun to go without lunch, but that doesn't give her the right to take out her frustrations on you. End by telling her that you know she's smart and that she'll figure out how to make sure she doesn't forget her lunch again.

Catch Her Being Wonderful

You are no longer going to be the spoiler, so you will need to be loving without being soft. When you were a spoiler, both you and your child may have confused love with your giving her what she wants or overprotecting her. Now she isn't going to get what she wants, and she will equate that with "You don't love me anymore," even if she doesn't say it out loud. She's going to need to hear you tell her how much you love her and how wonderful you think she is. The more often and varying the situations you tell her that in, the more powerful it will be. If you only tell her at bedtime, or only when she's behaving, it won't feel as unconditional to her as it needs to be. Catch her being charming, and tell her how much you love her at random times. Do it consistently after disciplining her. Make it fun and often so that it fills her world.

My oldest child is my only daughter. She's very social; quite serious, yet fun-loving; and sometimes her own worst enemy. Disciplining her was easy relative to her brothers, as she had often done all the work before I even had a chance to. I remember her at three, just having stolen a toy from her brother. She brought the toy to me and let me know that she wasn't able to share, but that she shouldn't get to play with it either since she was being mean to her brother. It was hard not to let her completely off the hook just for the adorable factor alone. I told her that I would help her by giving the toy to her brother, and that I would watch as she found something else to do that was just as fun. I also told her what a sweet sister she was and that it was okay that she wanted the toy, but not okay to take it from him. I needed to let her know at that moment that I loved her, even though she had been naughty. She was feeling very bad about herself and needed to know that I still found her very lovable.

Other children are more happy-go-lucky and seem fulfilled without frequent reassurance. Don't be fooled. Keep showering them with love and affection anyway. You may get, "I know, Mom, you don't have to tell me anymore." Just smile and let them know you can't help it, you just are so full of love that it has to spill out sometimes. They don't have a love meter, and you can't tell when they're running low until they're way too low. To avoid emergencies, make sure they are topped off.

Show Her That You Can Be Calm and Reasonable

Role-modeling is essential to establishing yourself as the rock. She needs to see how you handle it when you have behaved badly. One of the biggest mistakes I have seen in parenting is when someone refuses to admit that they are wrong or that they made a mistake. Somehow this parent thinks that admitting the mistake makes them seem weak. Even very young children can smell a rat. You can't expect your child to admit her mistakes and say she's sorry if you won't. She may cooperate with you out of fear or obligation, but her trust in you will be damaged if you try to pretend that you are perfect.

If she has witnessed you cursing at the driver who just cut you off, come clean, even if she doesn't say anything. Admit that you didn't need to act so poorly and that maybe the other driver just made a mistake or had an emergency to take care of. Wouldn't you want other drivers to be courteous and generous when you make a mistake? She will learn how to handle situations in her own life from your good example.

As a rock, you want to provide a role model for emotional control when angry, for empathy with those who have treated you badly, for how to be a good friend, for self-discipline, etc. In short, exemplify all the things that you want for your child. You can't eat cookies for breakfast and then expect her to appreciate her eggs and toast. Be emotionally honest with your child and show her how an adult behaves. She'll learn more by watching than listening.

When you decide to be the rock, your child is going to do everything in her power to wear you down and break your resolve. But you're a rock, and it takes hundreds of years to break down a rock. You are going to implement the basics, shower her with love, be a calm and reasonable role model and discipline consistently. And it's going to take a while. She could manipulate you before, and you caved in then; so she's thinking maybe it'll just take a little more effort now. She'll pull out all the stops, but she's up against the rock. You will win, I promise.

15

Is This the Hill to Die On?

Being the rock is about keeping your emotions under control and modeling mature behavior so that your child knows he can always count on you to guide, nurture and protect him. It's easier to be the rock when you reframe your expectations from being surprised and angered by his misbehavior to knowing that he will act up from time to time, and when you have the confidence that you can parent him calmly when that happens. Now that you are the rock and your child knows you mean business, you can set the foundation for the key element of discipline – consistency.

Consistency Is Not as Fun as Making Your Child Happy in the Moment

If you have struggled with being consistent, you are not alone. Let's face it, in the moment it's easier to cave in than stand your ground with your child. When you stand your ground, you have to be prepared for your child to be unhappy with you. It is not one of the most immediately rewarding or pleasant parenting tasks.

Just This Once

In addition, you may be the kind of parent who feels there is no harm in giving in once in a while. You rationalize, "What's the big deal?" Let's say he's screaming for a cookie that you told him he cannot have in the store at 2:00 in the afternoon. However, you may feel guilty because you woke him up early from his nap. So you cave in and give him the cookie. This makes him happy, keeps him quiet and assuages your guilt over interrupting his nap. You rationalize that "just this once," it will be fine.

Justification is extremely powerful. However, giving in on occasion teaches your child that you don't mean what you say. If he doesn't believe you, you will struggle even more to maintain consistency because he will challenge you more. You may be able to justify one cookie, just this once, but if you are honest with yourself you must admit that caving in is not good for your child's character development. You can't pretend that it is an effective or appropriate parenting technique.

You Are Frustrated That Your Child Doesn't Listen and Comply

Most parents of entitled children are enormously frustrated and overwhelmed. Your child has developed the skills and weapons he needs to wear you down. Standing your ground only to cave eventually exhausts valuable emotional resources. It's tough to say no to an entitled child. Even worse, if you say no and then eventually cave in, you spend a great deal of emotional energy with the letdown of a poor outcome. It's how many women feel when, after laboring in pain for hours and hours, they are informed by the obstetrician that they need to have a Cesarean section. The effort feels wasted.

Your lack of consistency has led you to conclude that discipline doesn't work

The more inconsistent you are, the more your child will escalate his behavior, because he knows that you will cave eventually. If he has no hope that you will give in, he might act up here and there; but he won't attempt a sustained naughty campaign because he knows that his effort would be wasted. He doesn't like no pain, no gain scenarios either. Your discipline has not worked, but you have reached the wrong conclusion about why that is the case. It hasn't worked because you have been inconsistent with your discipline, not because discipline itself doesn't work or because your child in particular cannot be disciplined.

Disciplining and rewarding children with the goal of encouraging or eliminating behaviors is known as "operant conditioning." You don't have to know the term or understand the science behind it to know that it works. Using stickers to reward good behavior and time-outs to discipline bad behavior are common examples of operant conditioning. However, there is an element of operant conditioning that many parents are unaware of. Inconsistency, or randomly applying a consequence when trying to eliminate a bad behavior, is actually very effective at reinforcing it. If you are inconsistent with discipline, you influence your child's behavior in exactly the opposite way than you intend to. No wonder you are frustrated!

I've heard many parents claim that time-outs don't work. When I hear this, I am fairly sure that I'm talking to a parent who has a problem with consistency. If you are giving your adult child money to bail him out again, letting your whiny child have his way and stay up past bedtime because you are too exhausted to deal with it for the third time this week, or figuring it won't hurt to buy your child the treat he's begging for at the store just this one time for the hundredth time, you are reinforcing his whining, begging and spendthrift ways.

You are frustrated and may feel like nothing works, when it is the inconsistent application of the discipline that has not worked. Now that you know you have to be consistent and that your child can learn what you have to teach him, you have the opportunity to teach him something new.

Clear Expectations

Expectations are tricky because they can result in miscommunication and confusion if not clearly defined and understood. To help facilitate the communication of your expectations to your child, it is helpful to divide them into two different types. Those that belong in the first category, which I will call non-negotiables, support your values. They are not meant to direct specific conduct. Expectations that fall into the second category are the actions specifically requested or outlined so that your child knows what specific behavior you require of him. Both kinds of expectations need to be communicated clearly by you and understood by your child, so that he can succeed in obeying you.

An example of a non-negotiable expectation would be, "I expect you to dress in an appropriate manner." Your child may see baggy pants or jeans with holes that show his underwear as fashion statements. He can only cooperate with your expectations if you further clarify how you define appropriate dress and develop directions that he can follow, such as no baggy pants that fall more than two inches below your belly button and no jeans with holes above the knees.

So what would be a non-negotiable? My children were aware of our house rules from an early age.

1) You must always tell the truth

2) You may not hurt others

3) Your job as a child is to be a student and get an education

4) You are expected to help out with chores

5) You may not take drugs or alcohol

6) You may never get in a car with someone who has taken drugs or alcohol

It's a pretty short list. You may be thinking that "Be respectful" should be on it. I took it off because it wasn't clear enough. A child sweeping the floor after dinner with a grumpy attitude could be breaking that rule, but he is still getting his chores done. I can overlook the fact that he's unhappy as long as he gets them done and isn't being hurtful or lashing out. Rolling eyes is an involuntary maneuver for teenagers and is not particularly respectful. If being respectful is a non-negotiable, you're going to need to spell out what applies and discipline consistently – this won't be easy if the category is too broad or ill-defined. What will the consequence be for eye-rolling? Pick your own rules, but be careful to think them through and figure out how to make them clear or they will be worthless.

Also, be careful to limit the list. If you have too many rules, it will be too easy for him to break at least one on any given day. If you have rules like, "Keep your room clean" or "Start your homework thirty minutes after you get home," you will be compelled to discipline when common sense says you may not have chosen to given the particular situation. For example, if your child comes home extremely upset that his best friend betrayed him by asking his girlfriend out, he may be too distressed to be effective at completing his homework. It may make more sense to go for a walk with him and give him some emotional support rather than enforce a thirty-minutes-to-start homework rule.

You may think having a long list of rules will make things easier, but it will make things harder. You want to gain his cooperation, not compel his behavior. With a long list, you will have too many instances where you're catching him doing something wrong. You want to provide lots of positive feedback and be able to give your child attention for the things he is doing well. Leaving the rule broad, such as my non-negotiable #3 (Your job as a child is to be a student and get an education) is much easier to enforce than "You must start your homework within thirty minutes after you get home from school." The point is that you want him to do his homework with adequate diligence without having to be reminded. Work with him to figure out the best way for him to be successful in accomplishing that task. Some kids need to run and get their energy out first. Some need a power snack. Others need to unwind with some friend time on the phone or a thirty-minute cartoon. A few like to get it over with and just need a quiet place the second they get home from school. If you have more than one child, they will probably have different needs. How he gets it done is less important than the fact that he does a good job and is responsible. Don't structure it too tightly or he will only be doing it because he has to –

which will not make him responsible about getting his work done now or when he has a paying job.

With the everyday expectations, you have to be careful about setting up a laundry list of rules or being so black-and-white that your child is always in trouble. The goal is not to be harsh and unyielding; it is to be consistent and make sure he follows the non-negotiable rules. Remember that inconsistency actually reinforces the behavior that you are trying to eliminate. A fear of being too strict or harsh is what keeps many parents from providing consistent discipline. You can have one without the other!

For example, you have established a bedtime of nine p.m. for your fifth-grader. You've had a busy night and he's been dying to show you a video of his class play all night. By the time you get a chance to see it, it will not have finished playing until after nine. You can choose to enforce bedtime and make a promise to watch it the next night. However, if your child has been very cooperative and has already brushed his teeth and is ready for bed, you could make an exception. As long as the exceptions don't become routine and you make it clear that his good behavior has earned him the exception, you can be flexible without causing a problem.

Making exceptions or being flexible may sound very similar to "just this once," or giving in when your child is acting up. The key difference is that you are making an exception in response to a specific circumstance or request, not as a reaction to misbehavior. If you notice he is starting to fight you on his bedtime, you will know you have not been consistent enough or have been making exceptions in response to bad behavior ("just this once"), and you can correct the situation before it escalates into bedtime wars every night.

Bedtime should never be a non-negotiable, because there will be times that you will want to make an exception to reward behavior and times when it's just not possible to enforce the rule without giving up too much. For example, there might be a little league game that runs late, a community event that is held on a school night, or a family celebration that is important for your family to enjoy. If bedtime is non-negotiable except when you say so, then it's not non-negotiable.

So the point is, be consistent. It's either negotiable or it's not. If it's a non-negotiable, you can never ever say yes, you can only decide that maybe it's really not a non-negotiable and take it off the list. If it's negotiable, you can say yes as long as you give thoughtful consideration to the rule. If your child starts abusing the flexibility and pestering you constantly, then you'll need to structure the rules more cleanly for that child, at least for a period of time. You can give him the message that pestering you is going to get him a result opposite of what he wants. Say no when he pesters, and give him a treat of an extra fifteen minutes on a night when he's been cooperative and hasn't pestered. You can also set limits to the exceptions – whatever will help set boundaries and still provide the flexibility you both need. Bedtime is rarely flexible in our home, but on occasion an extra few minutes are allowed, and it's a special time that brings us closer together.

Clear consequences

Once you and your child have a clear understanding of the non-negotiable list and everyday expectations, it will be his job to test you and your job to discipline him and establish logical consequences when (not if) he chooses to disobey.

Very young children are not good candidates for discipline

because they cannot fully grasp the difference between right and wrong. For children under two years old, the best strategy involves a good offense: provide plenty of interesting and safe opportunities for your child to play. However, you cannot entertain him every minute of the day, so you need to have some strategies for when he gets into mischief. Distraction is the best method to redirect your child when he is misbehaving. You can move his location, start singing, hand him his favorite toy – anything to move his attention away from what's getting him into trouble. You should tell him your expectation as you provide the distraction, so that he'll hear it many times before he will be expected to obey. For example, tell him, "You may not climb on the counter because it is not safe," as you move him to his train table and say, "I see the engine in the train station, do you?" Even though he may not be able to do what you ask him to right now, he will, through repetition, be able to remember and cooperate when he is older. Some older babies start to get frustrated when their wants get more sophisticated than their verbal skills. If your son is acting out and seems frustrated, help him to verbalize what he is feeling. For example, my youngest was crying in his room and tearing his toy box apart. I asked him if he was upset because he couldn't reach his toy and offered to help him. He calmed down immediately and put all his toys back in the toy box.

According to the American Academy of Pediatrics, time-outs can be effective for children over two years of age if used consistently for appropriate time periods without overusing the technique, and there is a strategy in place for managing escape behavior.[20] There are

---

[20] Committee on Psychosocial Aspects of Child and Family Health, "Guidance for Effective Discipline," American Academy of Pediatrics official Web site, "About AAP Policy" page, http://aappolicy.aappublications.org/cgi/content/full/pediatrics;101/4/723 (accessed February 15, 2012).

training programs available if you find you are not able to discipline your child effectively with time-outs. Your pediatrician would be an excellent resource for tips and guidelines. An effective time-out process looks like this:

1) Set up the time-out with a proper warning
2) Follow through with the warning if the behavior continues
3) Make sure you enforce the time-out
4) Manage escape behavior
5) Reinforce the time-out by repeating your expectation
6) Give your child affection

Giving more than one warning, keeping your child in time-out beyond what is age-appropriate and talking too much or over-explaining are all common mistakes that reduce or destroy the efficacy of the time-out.

Once your child responds less to time-outs (typically around age eight, give or take a couple of years depending on the child), you can restrict privileges or apply logical consequences instead. You will know time-outs are not as effective when he really doesn't mind the quiet time anymore. An older child will respond to logical consequences, such as not having the privilege of going out with his friends for a week or two because he broke curfew. If he lies to you, you will trust him less, be less likely to leave him unsupervised and do more to fact-check what he tells you.

What values did you identify in Chapter 13? If you don't already have them clearly defined, take a moment to identify the nonnegotiable expectations for your family that support your values.

Be particularly careful to make sure that each item on the list is something you can enforce one hundred percent of the time. Once everyone is clear on the non-negotiable list, then you can work with your family to cooperate on a daily basis with behaviors that support your family's values and expectations. Although it will take some time, with more clarity there will be fewer disagreements and a new spirit of cooperation. You will no longer feel the need to give in for momentary peace because you will have experienced the long-term benefits of being consistent.

16

You Can't Have Your Cake and Wear
Your Skinny Jeans Too

Through your family values and consistent discipline, you have
created a strong set of boundaries and limits for your child. This
foundation is critical to helping her understand the link between
responsibility and privilege. These limits help her accept and
appreciate responsibility, which must occur before she can
understand any link with privilege.

Linking responsibility and privilege together is critical for two
reasons. First, if you fail to link them and she can get everything she
wants without having to take responsibility, she will never be
responsible. The second is that privileges are a more powerful and
lasting motivator than consequences, and will carry her into
adulthood. If she is motivated by privileges, she is more likely to
make good decisions than if she is just avoiding consequences.

She Needs You to Set Boundaries

The limits you have set are important because in setting them, you communicate to your child that you care, she is safe and secure, and she can rely on you. She knows at some level that she lacks the maturity and understanding to take care of herself on her own. You aren't likely to hear her admit that – in fact, she will more likely let you know that she doesn't need you to tell her what to do. Remember how you felt as a child, when you were mad enough to run away from home only to turn back at the corner when the realities of fending for yourself started to sink in? Although she won't admit it, she needs you to set limits or she will lack the confidence to challenge herself and develop her abilities. If you fail to set limits, she will act out and keep pushing to find the perimeter which will include risky and dangerous behavior if left unchecked.

Boundaries and limits define ownership and responsibilities. In setting age-appropriate boundaries, you teach her to make good decisions and accept responsibility. For example, most young children can't wait to devour their candy on Halloween night. We parents know that if our child eats too much, it will affect her mood and energy level and may even cause her to get sick. When she was very young, you had to set the limits for her by giving her a few pieces and putting the rest out of sight. By setting the limits, you teach her about moderation and encourage her to make good choices on her own over time.

Helping your child to clearly understand the link between responsibilities and privileges – or more broadly, cause and effect – requires consistent discipline with firm boundaries, and then takes it one step further. We all want to have our cake and eat it while wearing our skinny jeans. If only life was really like that.

Ideally, this link needs to be firmly established for your child prior to age eight, when you are still the center of her universe and the smartest person she knows. It's never too late to teach your child this important life skill, but it will be more difficult the older she gets. Teaching the link later in life involves a lot more trial and error on your child's part and can be very painful for you to watch while you resist the temptation to rescue her.

So why is this hard? Because you don't want your child to be disappointed or hurt. It's tough to let your child make a poor choice and then suffer the consequences or be denied something she wants. You swoop in to protect her from temporary pain only to sentence her to a lifetime of frustration.

Cause and Effect

I'm not a huge fan of completely baby-proofing a house, because it shields your child from learning cause and effect. Making sure your child isn't physically hurt is important, but if you pad every corner, cover every outlet and hide everything not made of plastic, you have created a false environment. Along with no opportunity to get hurt, she has no opportunity to learn about dangers. She needs to know that if she runs with reckless abandon in a house, she may trip and fall against the coffee table and that it will hurt. She will learn to be more aware of her surroundings and a little more careful. In a padded home, she'll learn that she has no responsibility for her own safety. This works well at home, but not so well when you go visiting or are in public places.

I was recently at the library and witnessed a two year-old running and yelling at the top of his lungs. He was having a great time, and I love to see an exuberant and happy child, but not without limits. His mother was racing around after him, saving him from spills and repeatedly asking him to lower his voice and be careful, all from the moment they walked in to the moment they left. I was working to keep my sigh of relief private when I realized that others were not so inclined, and commenting on the brat that just left. My frustration was with the spoiler mom, who was likely on her way back to her baby-proofed home to rest up from her exhausting experience at the library.

Even babies can make the connection between cause and effect when parents expect them to. My youngest at two years old clearly knew what "hot" is and that he wants no part of anything hot. He flirted with touching the stove enough that he has an inkling of how bad hot can be without getting hurt. I always stood right next to him and would not have allowed him to burn himself, but he was testing the limits and I wanted him to understand that he needs to not touch something hot because it hurts. It is my responsibility to teach him the limit, and ultimately it will be his responsibility to regulate his own behavior. Now he is savvy enough that he will point to a coffee cup, say "hot" and steer clear without needing to be told.

If you don't fully baby-proof your house, it's more work at first, and you have to be more vigilant. Once your child learns to protect herself, it's less work because she knows how to behave in non-padded places. This is well worth the effort for those of us who love to be out and about!

She May Not Always "Get It" At First

When your child understands cause and effect, she can begin to learn the link between responsibilities and privileges. This is one of the tougher lessons to teach, because you are attempting to get her to understand something she would rather not accept and from which you could completely (or at least temporarily) shield her if you choose. Just as you would rather eat cake wearing your skinny jeans, she would love to skip homework on her path to being famous and wealthy.

A child under ten is not likely to agree with you on the link between responsibilities and privileges. She wants to believe that she can skip eating vegetables and fruits and still have good health. You can't convince her otherwise for now, so you have to make the link more immediate. You also need to make sure that the responsibility comes before the privilege. She'll learn that she earns the privilege by behaving responsibly. She can have dessert if she eats her vegetables first.

She may eventually become famous and wealthy with no formal education. She also won't have any major ill effects from not doing her homework for a few days. To her, these are both reasons that she shouldn't have to do something as disagreeable as homework. She is too young to appreciate the long-term effects of slacking on her schoolwork. You clearly can't give up and let her neglect her education. You also aren't going to be able to make her understand how critical education is to her opportunities for success later in life. She may only do homework for now because you require her to, or because she knows that you think it is important and she respects you. That's okay. If you have taught her that homework is her responsibility and watching a half hour of cartoons is the privilege she will earn by doing it, that's all she needs to learn for now.

Let's take it to the food realm, where so many battles are fought and, unfortunately for kids, so many parents lose. Out of my four children, only my third was extremely picky. At eighteen months, after being open to trying a variety of foods and liking many of them, his food world reduced to four things: cheese, rice, crackers and apples. And they couldn't touch on his plate or be combined in any way. I struggled with feeding this child for a year before I stumbled upon what would ultimately be salvation for us both. We struck a deal where he had to try the food, but could spit it out if he didn't like it. He was responsible for taking a taste, and his privilege was that he would not be forced to eat it if it was yucky. He spit out a lot of food, but over time his taste buds expanded and were even delighted, from time to time, with a new taste that he never would have experienced because it looked too yucky to even try. I had responsibility in this deal too. My job was to present interesting food and to keep offering previously rejected food. I also was responsible for holding up my end of the deal, which was allowing him to spit out food if he didn't like it. My reward was that we celebrated each new "not yucky" food with great fanfare. My ultimate reward and privilege is that my child is healthy, did not develop poor eating habits and loves a variety of foods, even some that I find yucky, like salmon and lamb.

Cause and Effect When Your Child Is 0-10

Find a way to link responsibility and privilege in a way that your child can understand at her stage of development. For the under-ten children, don't worry about the big picture – she isn't capable of grasping that yet, so don't get stuck trying to get her to agree with you. She needs to understand that brushing her teeth is her responsibility. The privilege of a healthy mouth is beyond her current ability to grasp, but getting to listen to her favorite song

173

while she brushes or earning an extra bedtime story by brushing without a reminder are things she will appreciate. Be creative – you know what your child loves and what will motivate her.

Cause and Effect When Your Child Is 10-20

If you are just now taking your power back and the link between privileges and responsibilities has not been firmly established for your tween or teen child, now is the time. It won't be easy or fun, but it also won't get any easier. A child in this age group is better able to understand the relationship between privilege and responsibility, but not necessarily more willing to accept that she doesn't get to have one without the other. There are many ways to teach this, and you will need more than one strategy.

I think chores are an excellent teaching tool for establishing the link between responsibility and privilege. By helping out around the house, your child learns that someone has to work to provide for the meals, the clean clothes and a warm bed. In the beginning that someone was you, but by the time she reaches adulthood it will need to be her and it will be easier for her if she isn't slammed into the role as an eighteen year-old newbie. She'll tell you that she hates to do chores. Just tell her it's okay, you don't love to do them either, but everyone needs to help. If she's unwilling to help, then she'll need to forgo the fruits of everyone else's labor. Make it fun, don't hold her to adult standards and be consistent with consequences.

Chores are also a great opportunity to develop team spirit and build family unity. There's no reason for everyone but Mom or Dad to be watching TV and lounging when there are dishes to be done. If everyone pitches in, there's time for a game or a walk together with the dog. Rally the troops! Let's get the house clean this morning and we'll pack a picnic and take a hike this afternoon!

Using chores as a teaching tool is one way to teach your child the link between responsibility and privilege. Two other important techniques, which have been more fully described in previous chapters, include role-modeling responsible behavior (Chapter 14) and not rescuing your child (Chapter 12).

Role-modeling is particularly important when teaching the link between responsibility and privilege to your child. Do you live within your means, do you keep your word, and are you on time? If you overspend, do your parents rescue you by helping with the bills? Do you promise to help a friend move and then change your mind when an offer that is more fun comes along? Do you keep your appointments and show up on time, or do you often reschedule, cancel or flake out on commitments that you have made? Do you get your projects done or do you procrastinate until the last possible minute? Your child will see how you handle responsibility and what privileges you treat yourself to. You have to hold yourself to the same standard that you expect her to meet.

Making sure you don't rescue your child has been discussed before, and is particularly important when teaching the link between responsibility and privilege. A friend of mine, Elaine, offered the reward of a concert to her thirteen year-old daughter, Lauren, if she earned a B average on her report card. Elaine was a little nervous about buying the tickets because she did not see any extra effort from her daughter, but decided to get the tickets anyway because she was worried that she wouldn't be able to get them last-minute. Lauren's report card was a disaster, even worse than the previous trimester. I was shocked to learn that Elaine took Lauren to the concert. Elaine rationalized that she had the tickets anyway and would be throwing the money away if she couldn't resell them. She also felt bad about disappointing Lauren. It was Lauren's favorite band and she had been talking about going to the concert non-stop. Elaine knew her daughter didn't work to her potential, but told Lauren that she was proud of her effort anyway. Unless Elaine stops rescuing her, the chances are slim that Lauren will take her mother seriously or put in extra effort to earn a reward in the future.

Cause and Effect When Your Child is 20+

The link between responsibilities and privileges is inescapable in the adult world – it will be harder or impossible for you to bail your child out when she becomes an adult. If she wants the privilege of attending a concert, she will need to earn money. If she wants to look great in a bikini, she'll need to make healthy food choices and exercise. If she wants better friends, she will need to be a better friend. Her long-term happiness is dependent on her ability to be responsible and make good decisions. You don't do her any favors by coddling her when she's young, because you rob of the chance to mature and learn responsibility before the consequences are harsher and nobody is interested in treating her to privileges she hasn't earned.

17

Wait, Wait, It Will Be Great!

Once your child appreciates the link between responsibility and privilege, he will be more motivated to make good decisions and self-regulate his behavior, no longer expecting a reward that he does not earn. However, he is not accustomed to waiting for what he wants and will need to learn to tolerate, if not appreciate, delayed gratification. Without this skill, he will be unable to wait for his reward without becoming frustrated.

Why Help Him Tolerate Delayed Gratification?

Beyond the fact that you don't want to see him frustrated, why is the ability to tolerate delayed gratification a critical skill that needs to be developed in an entitled child? This skill does more than cure the "gimmes" or "I wannas," although that may be reason enough for many parents. It also teaches him to be grateful and helps him develop a good work ethic. By teaching him to tolerate frustration, he becomes more productive, at lower risk for self-medicating behaviors and more likely to develop his own interests.

Curing the Gimmes

The strategy for helping your child develop this skill depends on his age. Younger children will be less tolerant and less able to understand the concept, so you'll want to be age-appropriate. Promising a two year-old that he can save his pennies and buy the truck he is screaming for at the store will accomplish nothing. Not only does he have no concept of the value of money, he'll also forget about the truck before you even leave the store. All you need to do is let him know that just because he wants it does not mean you are going to buy it.

Talking about money and saving up will be more useful with an eight year-old; or you may want to talk to him about putting it on his Christmas list and waiting to see if Santa will bring him one. My third child really wanted a hat that he found at the mall. He is a naturally contented type of kid who doesn't ask for a lot, so his request got my attention. I talked to him about using his money to buy it, which he didn't want to do. It was a $32 hat, likely to get left on the playground or crushed in the bottom of the abyss that passes for his closet, so I didn't really want to buy it either. However, I went back the next day and bought it, and gave it to him two months later for his birthday. He was so excited and surprised! Seven months later he still has the hat and it hasn't been destroyed. He wouldn't have been nearly so excited had I purchased the hat for him that day at the mall, and he also learned that I won't buy him something just because he likes it.

Teens readily understand the value of money, and should be getting a firm grasp on the difference between wants and needs and learning to set priorities. They should be learning to work within a budget, whether or not they earn their own money. They will quickly learn that spending money on lunch at school instead of packing one from home for free seriously cuts into their ability to put gas in the car or go to the movies with their friends. How about all the wants that crop up in high school that all seem so terribly important to them? Limo for prom, class ring, letterman's jacket – the list goes on. For non-essentials, I usually offered to pay half of the expense and expected my children to earn the money or use savings for the other half. It's amazing how many times the "have to have" item was not so important if they had to spend their own money for it.

Your ability to help your adult child learn to tolerate delayed gratification is limited. Unless he gave up and moved back home, he is already experiencing the realities of life without your protection or intervention. Whether he is living with you or not, the best way to help him is to stop rescuing him. Find a way to encourage him without solving his problem. Let him know that you believe in him and that he will find a way to take responsibility for himself. If you save him from the consequences of his poor choices or behaviors at this age, you give him no reason to become independent and develop to his full potential.

Wealthier families struggle with this issue more than those with fewer financial resources. It's simply harder to say no and watch your child struggle when you can afford to bail him out. It has been said that unearned wealth retards ambition. That certainly doesn't mean that all affluent families produce entitled children with an acute case of the gimmes, but they are more at-risk. We have all seen the struggles of pampered twenty-something celebrities who consistently seem to find a way to top their own outrageous behavior.

Warren Buffet, widely known as one of the most successful investors in the world and one of America's wealthiest individuals, has publicly stated that his children will not inherit his fortune. In a Fortune Magazine article titled, "Should I Leave It All To The Children?" Buffet's emphatic answer is "no." "To him the perfect amount to leave children is 'enough money so that they would feel they could do anything, but not so much that they could do nothing.'"[21]

For all age groups, the solution to curing the gimmes lies in parents' ability to help their children understand that they won't get what they want without earning it. How you do this varies with the age of your child, but you should be aware of wants versus needs and be sure to have him wait for or work for the extras.

Instilling a Good Work Ethic

Curing the gimmes is not the only reason for teaching your child the value of delayed gratification; it's also needed to learn a good work ethic. Without the patience to keep working before he experiences the results he is seeking, he won't sustain the effort. And that's when he has control over the outcome. Learning that great effort does not always produce favorable or desired results is hard for anyone and can be particularly devastating to a child accustomed to instant gratification. He'll likely be the one to justify his own lack of effort using one or two poor results as the excuse.

Encouraging him to volunteer for charitable causes, have regular contact with extended family members who can serve as good role

---

[21] Richard I. Kirkland, Jr., "Should You Leave It All to the Children?" *Fortune Magazine* (September 29, 1986).

models, turn off the television and video games and spend one night a week with the family are all good ways to help foster a healthy respect for money and hard work.

If you have an unmotivated child who is seriously performing below his potential, think about his need for instant gratification. Regardless of the age of your child, you can have a major influence on his chances for success by cutting off the gravy train.

For example, I have a friend, Carmen, who is heavily involved in her children's homework. She supervises study sessions, reviews assignments, plans project timelines and even organizes her kids' backpacks. She reasons that if she doesn't help them they will get poor grades, which will affect their ability to get into a good college. Her children rush through their homework knowing that mom will check it, allowing them to make minimal effort without the threat of a poor grade. They play video games while she sorts through their backpacks, taking out old papers and making sure they have everything they need for the next day. Carmen fails to see why her children do not put more effort into their schoolwork, given that she is working so hard to help them. She is failing to teach them that they need to put in the effort to earn good grades on their own.

Earning the privilege of having a family pet can help young children learn to tolerate delayed gratification. I know a family who graduated through pets until they got the puppy their children so desperately wanted. They started with a goldfish and stayed at that level for over six months until their children learned to be responsible for feeding the fish and cleaning the bowl regularly. After a turtle, a hamster and a bird, the family brought a puppy home. The children were elated, appreciative and diligent in caring for all the family pets.

Learning to Tolerate Frustration

Is your child easily irritated or unable to tolerate even the most minor frustrations? Is he more likely to seek pleasure or avoid pain in the moment, regardless of the long-term consequences?

For example, your child has a low frustration tolerance when he seems less and less impressed with gifts and surprises and it gets increasingly difficult to please him. He may open a birthday gift and make a comment like, "I wanted the blue one," or "This is crap now that the new version came out last week." The thrill is gone, because your child believes he can get anything he wants without having to wait.

Think back to a time when you really wanted something – like a bike for your birthday. You dream of the color it might be. You draw pictures as clues for your parents and leave them around the house for months. You even think about riding down the street on your brand-new bike with the streamers flying. Then the big day arrives and you get snow skis instead. Momentarily, you are crushed – you had so wanted that bike, and just knew that your life would be the best ever if only you had it. But you don't give up hope. You keep the dream alive and continue to leave clues and hints. Maybe you even take on a newspaper route or open a lemonade stand to earn some money so that you can buy the bicycle for yourself. Christmas comes and goes and still there's no bike. You keep hoping and keep working, and then the miracle happens on your next birthday. The bike is beautiful, and it even has a bell and water bottle attached. You are so excited that you can't stand it. You ride your bike for days on end and can't get enough of showing it off to your friends.

Your entitled child has been robbed of this experience – and if you were raised by spoiler parents, you were as well. Your child has been taught to believe that waiting or working for something he wants is a painful experience to be avoided. In addition, because he hasn't had to wait, he doesn't respect or appreciate what he gets.

Your entitled child has experienced high return for minimal effort. As he gets older, he will become increasingly frustrated when those outside his immediate family are uninterested in pampering him. Teachers, coaches, peers and friends will not reward him for his lack of effort the way you have. The next chapter focuses on helping your child to develop coping skills and self-regulation. For the rest of this chapter, I would like to spend a little time on an issue that the parent of every teen will face. It will be of increased concern for the parent of an easily frustrated child who may turn to substance abuse in an attempt to self-medicate.

Taking a Stand on Alcohol and Drugs

As reported by Students Against Destructive Decisions (SADD) using information from the National Institute on Drug Abuse, 72% of teens have consumed alcohol (more than a few sips) by the end of high school. The National Drug Intelligence Center (NDIC) reports that 40.2% of respondents in the ninth to twelfth grades had used marijuana at least once.[22] For some parents these numbers seem overwhelming, and many decide not to fight the inevitable.

If there was ever an issue to take a stand on, this may be the one. NDIC found a strong correlation between early drug use and adult dependence. Those who started using drugs at an earlier age were at an increased risk compared to those who first started after age eighteen. Further, "teens who first used marijuana before age 17

---

[22] SADD official Web site, "Stats" page, January, 2011, http://www.sadd.org/stats.htm (accessed February 15, 2012).

were shown to have smaller brains and to be physically smaller in height and weight than teens who first used marijuana after age 17. Exposure to marijuana and other drugs at certain critical periods, such as early adolescence, may alter normal patterns of development."[23]

Make sure your child knows the dangers and that you will not allow him to expose himself to them. Does this mean that he won't try? Of course not, but you shouldn't buy alcohol or drugs for him and invite his friends over. And if he does experiment, treat it like the broken rule that it is. If it happens more than once or twice, take him to professionals for treatment immediately. Why would you want your child to take such a destructive chance with his brain and his future? If he learns to self-medicate with drugs and alcohol, he won't learn healthy ways to relieve stress and anxiety.

Don't use the excuse that he'll go crazy in college if you don't let him drink or use marijuana while he's in your home and you can still protect him. You can't protect his body and brain from the damage; you can only make sure he doesn't get into a car and immediately hurt himself or someone else. Worst case, if he does experiment heavily or become addicted in college, he'll be older and his brain more mature. He will have gained critical years without the destructive effects and he'll have a better chance at a life free of addiction.

So if he can't drink, does this mean you can't either? This is a tough one for many parents, but I feel that children need to learn the lesson that adults have privileges that they do not. Alcohol fits into

---

[23] National Drug Intelligence Center, "Teens and Drugs: Fast Facts," Product No. 2004-L0559-011, archived January 1, 2006, official U.S. Department of Justice Web site, http://www.justice.gov/ndic/pubs11/12430/index.htm (accessed February 15, 2012).

that category. You can't drive until you are sixteen, and you have to be eighteen to vote or sign a contract. You need to be mature enough to appreciate the risks and accept the consequences if you make a poor choice. Having a glass of wine with dinner or a cocktail with friends on a weekend can be fun and part of your world. Having teens doesn't mean you need to give that up, it just means that you need to be setting a good example by using alcohol responsibly. They will be exposed to it, and they need to know that it can be a fun part of the social experience without being problematic. Drugs, on the other hand, are illegal. Without debating that issue, you can't legally possess or use drugs. Keep it out of the house and set the good example. It's what you signed up for when you became a parent, and your child is depending on you.

Teach Him to Wait

It often seems as if half our lives are spent in lines or waiting for someone. The term "road rage" was coined in the late 1980s, as traffic congestion increased and frustrated drivers resorted to extreme acts of aggression in response. Traffic congestion is simply waiting in line while behind the wheel. If you have been chased down, swerved at, or given "the finger," you have experienced the road rage phenomenon. Why are people behaving so badly and so unable to tolerate this everyday frustration? Entitled children are not the only group of people who lack this skill, but the ability to wait, delay gratification and tolerate frustration is a lesson they in particular have not been taught and need to learn to be successful.

You child needs to allow for other people to make mistakes, and to understand that his needs do not rise in importance above everyone else's and he will be fine if he has to wait for what he wants. To review, the following strategies are useful in teaching your child to tolerate frustration and delayed gratification:

1) Do not give him everything he wants

2) When you do decide to treat him, don't always give it to him immediately

3) Require him to earn or work for what he wants

4) Do not rescue him from the consequences of his own behavior

5) Use chores as a teaching tool to help him develop a good work ethic

6) Involve him in volunteer work

7) Encourage him to solve his own problems

8) Give him plenty of opportunity to spend time with the family, extended family and friends who can serve as positive role models

9) Turn off the television and video games on a regular basis to encourage interaction

You may be surprised at what happens when you step back and make the changes listed above. His frustration level may increase initially, but as he learns to solve his own problems and adjust his effort to produce the outcome he desires, he will feel more confident and secure. You won't feel the temptation to rescue him as often because he will create fewer messes. Instead of rescuing, what he really needs is your encouragement and affirmation that he is capable and able to work out his own problems.

18

Coping Skills That Make a Difference

My favorite coping skill is taking a candle-lit bath while reading a great book. Even if my day was rough, the job stressful and the household chaotic, I can escape and really relax for a few minutes. After a bath I am kinder and gentler, even if the world is not. We all experience stress on a daily basis. Coping skills are the tools we use to manage our own behavior. You need to teach your child healthy coping skills, or she will either fail to self-regulate or develop unhealthy coping skills.

After clearly communicating your values, providing calm and consistent discipline and teaching your child the link between responsibility and privilege and how to tolerate delayed gratification, she will still occasionally get frustrated and angry (hopefully with decreasing frequency). This isn't a failure on your part; it's simply how life works. The last solution to help your child transition from entitled to enchanting involves teaching her coping and self-regulation skills.

Before you begin teaching her skills, it is critical that you role-model the behavior you expect from her. It is imperative to stay calm and responsible under difficult circumstances – be the rock! You can't lose your cool, yell at her and then expect her to behave.

Also critical will be setting appropriate limits (as outlined in Chapter 15), by establishing clear expectations and consequences and providing consistent discipline. For a minor child, having boundaries set by a parent creates predictability, which in turn provides a secure environment for her to develop and explore in. Without boundaries she will feel less structured internally, making it less likely that she will be successful at regulating her own behavior.

If you did not set limits and provide consistency before your child reached adulthood, she will be less adept at managing her behavior, and you are not going to be able to regulate it through discipline. Instead, your ability to set boundaries must focus on setting limits on the behavior you are willing to support and tolerate. If she torments the entire family with her demands and poor behavior during a holiday gathering, tell her that if she doesn't conduct herself respectfully, she won't be invited next time. You can't compel her to behave, but you can teach her that you won't willingly subject yourself to her bad behavior.

Self-regulation and coping skills are important because you can't protect her from frustration and disappointment. She needs to learn how to manage through difficult situations without misbehaving or losing her cool. With these skills, she will feel more confident and independent, and behave more appropriately.

Teach Her to Manage Frustration

Helping your child to manage her frustration begins with noticing what's going on. For example, if your seventh-grader studied diligently all week for a major history test only to receive a D mark, help her verbalize what she is feeling. She may try to brush it off with "I don't care," or "It doesn't matter how hard I try, I can't get a good grade anyway." The truth is, she studied hard and got a poor result. That is truly frustrating. She will be better able to cope with disappointment if you teach her to face it. Validate her feelings. Let her know that it's okay to be frustrated.

Once she has had a chance to vent, encourage her to think about solutions, providing support as appropriate for her age. She may need to study with other students, get tutoring if she is behind or check in with the teacher for suggestions. She will feel less frustrated if she is able to find ways to positively impact her situation. You should refrain from telling her what to do – that will confirm her belief that she can't earn a passing grade on her own. Spend time with her, listen to her and resist the urge to fix her problem for her.

Coping Skills

Sometimes, a frustrating or unpleasant situation cannot be avoided. We just have to get through it. For one of my children, a visit to the dentist falls squarely into this category. Your child needs coping skills to be able to get through those situations that are disagreeable or downright offensive.

Deep breathing and counting to ten are techniques that work well, because they force a pause or break from stress. Once she is focused on her breath or on counting, your child will give herself time to calm down and be able to think more rationally. Teach her to focus on her breath, breathing in deeply through her nose and out through her mouth. Her body will physically relax as she continues to breathe, which will help her feel more emotionally relaxed as well.

Keeping a journal is a positive coping skill for many children, particularly for those who feel misunderstood. A journal is like a best friend – one that never tells a secret. The ability to write down crushes, disappointments and dreams without fear of judgment or retribution is very relaxing and provides a safe outlet.

Distractions such as physical exercise, drawing, listening to music or reading can serve as positive coping mechanisms as well. Physical distractions are particularly good for highly energetic children, or for extremely stressful situations. Good examples are biking, jumping on the trampoline, playing in the park, skateboarding, jumping rope and running. In addition to providing a distraction, physical activity produces endorphins, a substance which elevates feelings of well-being. Encourage your child to explore many activities so that she has many to choose from when she needs to manage stress. If there are physical activities that you enjoy and can do with her, such as tennis or rollerblading, giving her access to great coping skills and increasing the amount of time you spend with her is a double bonus!

One coping skill that is particularly effective and can be used almost anywhere within any time limitation is visualization. The ability to create a calming, pleasant place in her mind can provide your child with a break and a chance to regroup no matter where she is or what stress she is facing. Encourage her to think of the most relaxing time she can remember, and then to close her eyes and recreate it whenever she feels frustrated or stressed.

Your child will be soothed by some of these techniques, and find that others do not work for her. That's fine. We are all wired differently and what calms one may irritate another. The technique she uses to calm herself is less important than the fact that she can.

Avoid the frustration

The antidote to boredom, frustration, negativity and acting out ultimately lies within your child. She needs to be the one to regulate her behavior, conduct herself responsibly, be productive and appreciate what she has. It is wonderful to teach her coping skills, but even better to teach her how to reduce the need for them. If she has been coddled, overindulged or allowed to roam free, she does not have a clear vision of what it means to be responsible.

Occasionally, I have a friend ask me to meet with an adult child to provide financial guidance. There is usually an equal mix of frustration and concern from the parent who has an underachieving child still living at home.

The best example of this I've seen is Carly, a twenty-four year-old woman still living with her parents. She has over $2,000 in credit card debt and is working part-time as a waitress, not in school and dating a man with even more severe financial issues. In the first fifteen minutes of our conversation, Carly described herself as lazy, fat, spoiled and irresponsible. After hearing her describe herself in such unflattering terms, I repeated her words back to her and asked her if she truly believed that about herself. Her answer was that she hoped not, but she didn't know for sure because her parents had never expected anything better from her.

Carly's lesson is that our children are crying out for us to expect better from them. Society will expect better, and if we do not

191

prepare them for that, they will feel inadequate.

What Carly needed, and still needs, is to understand what being personally responsible means. Phil, a friend of mine who teaches children through the Junior Achievement® program,[24] has a simple and effective five-step process for this.

1) Be on time. The foundation of personal responsibility starts with showing up. The great coach Vince Lombardi, dedicated to instilling qualities of commitment and preparedness in his athletes, insisted that his players show up ready for practice ten to fifteen minutes early. The message here is that you need to put in extra effort and preparation before you can expect better results.

2) Do what you say. Any child can relate to the disappointment of being on the receiving end of a broken promise, so she'll relate to this one. She won't like to be promised a pizza lunch for a hard-earned grade only to hear excuses about a scheduling conflict. Help her turn her passion from being on the receiving end of a broken promise to being one who doesn't treat others that way.

3) Finish what you start. Can you imagine fireworks on the Fourth of July without the finale, or Thanksgiving dinner without the pumpkin pie? Any effort worth undertaking is worth completing.

4) Do more than what is expected. The lesson here is that you cannot expect better than average results if you are only willing to fulfill minimum requirements. Go the extra mile and you will be rewarded in return.

---

[24] Junior Achievement® official Web site, http://ja.org/ (accessed February 15, 2012).

5) Always maintain a great attitude! How people perceive you is as important as the delivery. Back up your effort with a positive delivery and you will multiply your chances at success.

Your child needs to know that you believe in her, and this will be easier if you feel more confident in her abilities because you have equipped her with the skills she needs. Role-model the way you would like her to behave, set appropriate boundaries and teach her coping skills.

Imagine the heartbreak of having a child who describes herself as Carly did. Lazy. Fat. Spoiled. Irresponsible. She knew the truth. She was raised by very loving parents who did her no favors by expecting very little from her and shielding her from even minor disappointment. She knows she can do better and is determined to step up. Her road would be much easier if her parents stepped up too, and became disciplined parents determined to stop their spoiling ways.

Part Four

A Word of Encouragement

19

It's Worth It!

My hope for those of you who are reading this book is that you have greater clarity about what spoiler parenting is, how it impacts you and your child, and what you can do to help your child and be a disciplined parent instead.

Important Reminders for Disciplined Parents

1) Your child needs you to be a disciplined parent – his happiness depends on it

2) You don't need his permission to change

3) He will escalate his behavior as you begin to make changes – expect his behavior to get worse before it gets better

4) Take care of yourself – this will be tough and you will need to practice healthy coping skills too

5) Get support from family, co-parents where possible, supportive friends and mental health professionals if necessary – don't feel like you are alone

6) Remind yourself of the bigger picture, and the fact that you

aren't willing to trade short-term peace for long-term happiness anymore

7) You and your child deserve it!

In the proceeding chapters, we explored the questions, "How did I get here, what did I do wrong, and what do I do now?" Even armed with knowledge, and knowing you are a spoiler and want to stop, facing that you have to try something new can be scary – even scarier if you know that you need to change but aren't sure you can. You will be facing your own fears, and the guilt you may feel for the way you have raised your child and how it is affecting him. In addition, your changes will trigger some discomfort for your child and your relationship with him will experience some stress.

Be as kind to yourself as you would be to your best friend or someone else you love. Make sure you are supported by and providing support to the other parental figures in your child's life. Reach out to friends or members of your community that you trust. If you have a church community, plug into the resources available there. Be sure your coping skills are in good repair and that you schedule in time for the things that allow you to rejuvenate. Consider professional counseling if you feel too overwhelmed or that you don't have the knowledge or skills you need to stop spoiling your child.

Your Child Needs You to Stop Spoiling Him

Here it is – the number one reason to step up, do your child a favor and put on your big parent pants. He deserves it. You have always wanted the best for him, and what is best is that you no longer spoil him. It's sometimes easier to just give him what he wants or just do it for him because you're afraid he'll mess up. But he can't live a fulfilled adult life with an umbilical cord wrapped around his neck.

I am seeing older and older children move back in with Mom and Dad. Catching up with a client, I found out that her sixty-two year-old son had moved back in. He had never been married, had no children, had lost his job and was drowning in credit card debt. She was wondering how much to help him out this time. Do you really want that for your child? Is protecting him from the smallest scrape or disappointment or unfulfilled wish so important once you understand that in doing so, you condemn him to a life of being needy? Even if you have all the financial resources to make him very comfortable, isn't it valuable for him to know that he can depend on himself?

And as comfortable as the status quo seems when compared with change and the unknown, neither you nor your child are happy. He wants more, you feel unappreciated. He feels deprived, you feel used. He feels you don't trust him, you feel like you can't trust him. And you both feel disrespected. The pain you are both feeling will only get worse unless you stop spoiling him.

One of the things that held you back in the past is that you have made brief attempts at taking your power back, and it has resulted in worse behavior and more tension. You have to expect that. It will get worse before it gets better. Neither of you can be happy as the spoiler and the spoiled, so be ready for the bumps in the road on the way to solving the problem.

Now you know why there is so much conflict in your relationship. Even though he's getting what he wants and you're giving in to his demands, it's never enough. He is unhappy despite having the ability to make his own decisions, knowing that you will protect him from the consequences. If you have given your power to him it's too much for him to handle, no matter how old he is. You're unhappy because you know you should not have relinquished your power to someone so ill-equipped to handle it, and you feel bad for giving him that burden. In trading security and peace in the moment for a lifetime of misery, you have been extremely shortsighted.

You Don't Need His Permission to Change from Spoiler to Disciplined Parent

What will happen if you take back your power now? Will he hate you? Maybe – but probably only for a while. The younger he is, the faster you will be able to heal the relationship. You have to be secure enough as a parent that you can do the right thing without needing his approval. You can let him know what you're doing and why you're doing it, but don't feel compelled to explain until you bring him around to your point of view, because that isn't likely to happen. Be willing to take a stand for his future even if it's uncomfortable for a while.

Statistically, it is unlikely that you will outlive your child. Even if it were healthy to keep him dependent on you well into adulthood, you can't be there for him forever. And, it's likely that at some point you are going to find it less appealing that your child depends on you so much. Co-signing for your twenty-four-year-old because he got himself into credit card trouble in college may have seemed okay, but it's less attractive when it's ten years later and you're still being asked to co-sign. Nothing has changed because there has been no need. Now it's a bigger loan, he's got more responsibilities and helping him could jeopardize your finances if he defaults because you're retired and have less disposable income. This scenario may seem farfetched, but it is all too common. Do your child a favor and don't co-sign the first time. If he's looking for ideas, suggest that he clean up his debt and buy an extremely cheap car for cash. If he's just looking for a handout, let him know that you aren't the one to help him. After he figures out how to buy a car without relying on someone else, he'll feel more capable and confident. What could be better?

If you are financially well-off, think about the legacy you want to leave with your child while you are making plans for when you are gone. Unearned wealth has immense power to corrupt and destroy, as discussed in Chapter 17. We've all heard of the lottery winners who go from rags to millions to rags in a very short period of time. Large inheritances can have the same impact as lottery winnings. Think carefully about how your child might handle a large windfall, and what safeguards you might put in place to preserve the value of your assets and spare him the potential of being burdened by an inheritance he may not be equipped to handle.

You have hurt your child by spoiling him. You have a choice – keep doing it and keep hurting him, or fix it. If you don't feel like you're strong enough, make sure to surround yourself with support. If you fear that your relationship with your child will be damaged, take a moment and realize that damage has already been done and you are taking a risk to make it better. There are never any guarantees. You can't keep hurting your child because you fear losing him. Better to lose him and hope that he comes back than completely ruin him by your own hand.

When you decide to put on your big parent pants, take back your power and give your child what he really needs despite your fears, you show him what responsibility and love are all about.

Resources

Here are some Web resources I've gathered to help support you and your child on your journey from spoiler and spoiled to disciplined and enchanting:

Love and Logic®: www.loveandlogic.com

Kids Health: www.kidshealth.org

Coping Skills for Kids Brain Works Project:
www.copingskills4kids.net

The International Network for Children and Families:
www.incaf.com

Junior Achievement®: www.ja.org

Dr. Jerry L and Sarah L Cook's Raising CEO Kids:
www.raisingceokids.com

Parent Further® – a Search Institute resource for families:
www.parentfurther.com

PARENTING Informed (good directory of resources here):
www.parentinginformed.com

American Academy of Pediatrics®: www.aap.org

Also powered by the American Academy of Pediatrics®:
www.healthychildren.org

Family Education (part of the Family Education Network):
www.familyeducation.com